Conscience: A Very Short Introduction

VERY SHORT INTRODUCTIONS are for anyone wanting a stimulating and accessible way into a new subject. They are written by experts, and have been translated into more than 45 different languages.

The series began in 1995, and now covers a wide variety of topics in every discipline. The VSI library now contains over 500 volumes—a Very Short Introduction to everything from Psychology and Philosophy of Science to American History and Relativity—and continues to grow in every subject area.

Titles in the series include the following:

AFRICAN HISTORY John Parker and
    Richard Rathbone
AGEING Nancy A. Pachana
AGNOSTICISM Robin Le Poidevin
AGRICULTURE Paul Brassley and
    Richard Soffe
ALEXANDER THE GREAT
    Hugh Bowden
ALGEBRA Peter M. Higgins
AMERICAN HISTORY Paul S. Boyer
AMERICAN IMMIGRATION
    David A. Gerber
AMERICAN LEGAL HISTORY
    G. Edward White
AMERICAN POLITICAL
    HISTORY Donald Critchlow
AMERICAN POLITICAL PARTIES
    AND ELECTIONS L. Sandy Maisel
AMERICAN POLITICS
    Richard M. Valelly
THE AMERICAN PRESIDENCY
    Charles O. Jones
AMERICAN SLAVERY
    Heather Andrea Williams
THE AMERICAN WEST Stephen Aron
AMERICAN WOMEN'S HISTORY
    Susan Ware
ANAESTHESIA Aidan O'Donnell
ANARCHISM Colin Ward
ANCIENT EGYPT Ian Shaw
ANCIENT GREECE Paul Cartledge
THE ANCIENT NEAR EAST
    Amanda H. Podany
ANCIENT PHILOSOPHY Julia Annas

ANCIENT WARFARE Harry Sidebottom
ANGLICANISM Mark Chapman
THE ANGLO-SAXON AGE John Blair
ANIMAL BEHAVIOUR
    Tristram D. Wyatt
ANIMAL RIGHTS David DeGrazia
ANXIETY Daniel Freeman and
    Jason Freeman
ARCHAEOLOGY Paul Bahn
ARISTOTLE Jonathan Barnes
ART HISTORY Dana Arnold
ART THEORY Cynthia Freeland
ASTROPHYSICS James Binney
ATHEISM Julian Baggini
THE ATMOSPHERE Paul I. Palmer
AUGUSTINE Henry Chadwick
THE AZTECS David Carrasco
BABYLONIA Trevor Bryce
BACTERIA Sebastian G. B. Amyes
BANKING John Goddard and
    John O. S. Wilson
BARTHES Jonathan Culler
BEAUTY Roger Scruton
THE BIBLE John Riches
BLACK HOLES Katherine Blundell
BLOOD Chris Cooper
THE BODY Chris Shilling
THE BOOK OF MORMON
    Terryl Givens
BORDERS Alexander C. Diener and
    Joshua Hagen
THE BRAIN Michael O'Shea
THE BRICS Andrew F. Cooper
BRITISH POLITICS Anthony Wright

Paul Strohm

CONSCIENCE

A Very Short Introduction

OXFORD
UNIVERSITY PRESS

OXFORD

UNIVERSITY PRESS

Great Clarendon Street, Oxford ox2 6DP

Oxford University Press is a department of the University of Oxford.
It furthers the University's objective of excellence in research, scholarship, and
education by publishing worldwide in

Oxford New York

Auckland Cape Town Dar es Salaam Hong Kong Karachi
Kuala Lumpur Madrid Melbourne Mexico City Nairobi
New Delhi Shanghai Taipei Toronto

With offices in

Argentina Austria Brazil Chile Czech Republic France Greece
Guatemala Hungary Italy Japan Poland Portugal Singapore
South Korea Switzerland Thailand Turkey Ukraine Vietnam

Oxford is a registered trade mark of Oxford University Press
in the UK and in certain other countries

Published in the United States
by Oxford University Press Inc., New York

© Paul Strohm 2011

The moral rights of the author have been asserted
Database right Oxford University Press (maker)

First published 2011

British Library Cataloguing in Publication Data

Data available

Library of Congress Cataloging in Publication Data

Data available

Typeset by SPI Publisher Services, Pondicherry, India

Printed and bound by
CPI Group (UK) Ltd, Croydon, CR0 4YY

ISBN 978-0-19-956969-4

Contents

Acknowledgements

For advice and criticism, I wish to thank Robert Alter, Akeel Bilgrami, Christopher Bradley, Andrew Cole, Katherine Cooper, Monica Corton, Holly Crocker, Anthony DeCurtis, Carolyn Dinshaw, Mikalina Efros, Jess Fenn, Claire Harman, Bruce Kogut, Lydia Liu, Maura Nolan, Laura Perille, Asia Rowe, Cathy Popkin, Miri Rubin, James Simpson, Abraham Stoll, John P. Strohm, Arvind Thomas, and David Wallace.

List of illustrations

Introduction

The variable yet durable phenomenon called conscience has
outlasted epochs and empires, credos and creeds, and has
influenced human behaviour for 2,000 years and more. The
Romans identified it (and named it: *conscientia*). The early
Christians appropriated it. Reformation Protestants and loyal
Catholics relied equally upon its advice and admonition. In the
17th and 18th centuries, it re-crossed the religious/secular divide,
shifting attention from religious perfection to ethical and social
betterment. Today, it is embraced with equal conviction by non-
religious and religious alike. It enjoys a privileged place in theology
and devotion, but no less in art and philosophy. Politicians claim
to act on its behalf, and occasionally do. Equally striking is its
breadth of appeal among all kinds and classes of persons: a subject
of rarified academic inquiry that works at street level too, and
is confidently cited by people in all walks of life as a basis for
their actions.

Conscience's astonishing persistence might seem to suggest that it
is a fixed entity, a unitary perspective unchanged across time. In
fact, conscience lives in time and its most prepossessing trait is a
capacity for constant self-modification and adaptation to new
circumstances, a limitless responsiveness to new and urgent
conditions of relevance. In this *Very Short Introduction*, I will treat

conscience not as an unvarying constant, but as a feat of human invention with a distinctive and eventful history all its own.

Conscience refuses any settled or unvarying content. It can justify generous self-sacrifice, but selfish individualism as well. It can motivate an act of charity or an act of terror. The dictates of conscience can be Christian or pagan, divinely based or resolutely secular, selfishly nationalistic or generously international. Even its gender remains uncertain: conscience may be male or female, a disembodied voice or a parental one, may even speak in chorus as public opinion. Equally variable with regard to source and location, conscience may be heard as a prompting voice within or as a commanding voice from without, and often both at once: an uncanny presence which knows everything about us yet retains an outside loyalty, whether to a deity or to the common good. Excellent things and some terrible things have been done in its name; much reasoned social betterment and occasional mad exceptionalism.

Conscience is, perhaps by definition, inconvenient. The individual visited by conscience usually feels, at least initially, that he or she was doing fine without it. Moreover, if conscience is variable with respect to its location or its content, some elements of what might be called its 'personality' remain distressingly the same. Wherever and whenever encountered, its characteristic habit is to goad, prick, wheedle, denounce, and harass rather than to mollify or assuage. If popular, it remains one of the least ingratiating of popular phenomena. The question, then, is why we need such an unpredictable and demanding and awkwardly stringent concept in our lives at all. The answer I will give is that we're far, far better off with conscience than without it.

Such an answer is best attempted, though, after more sustained thought about where conscience came from, who has sponsored it, and what it has meant to successive generations of people. It has deep historical roots, and renews and replenishes itself from those roots. Its best hope for future survival lies in an appreciation of this 'root system', consisting in all the things conscience has ever meant and been, as a basis for continuing and urgent applicability to the world today.

The cultural geography of conscience

Conscience has influenced persons of stature throughout the world, from the founders of the American republic through Gandhi and Mandela and beyond, but its origins (and still, to some extent, its sponsorship) are European and European-derived.

The West has no monopoly on ethical self-scrutiny or principled inner rejection of ethically repugnant behaviour. Certainly, all languages and all societies possess their own, distinctive conceptions of duty or responsibility, or shame about failure to meet the standards of the society or the self. Even though ancient Hebrew had no word or exact equivalent for conscience itself, Hebrew theology has gotten along perfectly well on concepts of will and intent and moral duty and responsibility before a God who implants precepts in the heart of the believer (Deuteronomy 30:14, Jeremiah 31:33). Although separate in origin, such Hebrew concepts as the divine injunction to moral self-scrutiny and the lodging of a moral faculty within the body have been indispensable to the development of Christian conscience and have served it as a conditioning influence and an absent cause. (Further enriching this exchange, Modern Hebrew now includes the word *matzpun*, which draws close to conscience in its etymological associations with interiority and also with the Hebrew word for 'compass'.) Greek *syneidesis*, an inherent and interior quality of ethical discernment, has traits in common with Christian conscience, and can indeed share with conscience a reflexive sense of self-knowledge, or knowledge of self by self. Buddhist and Hindu equivalents come closer to what modern English calls 'consciousness' than to 'conscience', but these were indivisible concepts in English until the 17th century, and sometimes thereafter. Conscience in Russian is *sovest*, a borrowing from Greek via Old Church Slavonic, and shares with conscience a sense of mutual knowing, either as self-reflexive awareness of knowing with another – etymologically, one may compare *con* (mutual) + *scientia* (knowledge) and *so-* (with) + *vest* (knowledge). Confucian concepts of *liangxin* (well-disposed feelings of heart/mind) and *liang zhi* (good moral thought or discernment) are tantalizingly similar to conscience in their emphasis on self-regulation and have enriched discussions of conscience in the 20th century. Arabic possesses the concept of *al-zājir*, or 'the restrainer', defined as 'God's preacher in the heart of the believer, the light cast therein which summons him to the truth', similar to conscience in its emphasis on prohibition of wrongdoing.

A medieval proverb describes 'many roads to Compostella', and these varied systems remind us that the goal of ethical self-scrutiny occurs outside as well as inside the tradition of conscience. Although operating similarly to conscience, these alternative systems are not its identical twins; each possesses subtleties and traditional differences that reward study in their own right. An earlier and patronizing Western liberalism offhandedly assumed that global ethical systems could be seamlessly identified with conscience, and that no significant differences need be acknowledged. Yet this turns out, especially in the context of proposed declarations of international conscience, or proposed intercultural initiatives to be taken in the name of 'conscience', not precisely to be the case. Cross-cultural respect is less well served by casual assertions of similarity than by appreciative attention to the distinctive features of each system.

A truly international comparatism is, of course, beyond the scope of this study, and beyond the limits of its author's knowledge. This study will focus on the particular traditions of conscience as it has developed over 2,000 years in the West. At *its* best and *our* best, conscience deserves its reputation as one of the prouder Western contributions to human dignity. It stands, as theologian Henry

Chadwick once commented, as a bulwark 'against the trivialisation of man'. As embodied in documents like the United Nations' *Universal Declaration of Human Rights* and as carried forward by organizations like Amnesty International and Human Rights Watch, it has much to offer to the discussion of human rights throughout the world. But, if it is to be considered for promulgation to other languages and cultures, then a sense of its historical development – including its abuses, blindspots, and contradictions – will encourage the proper humility with which to present this concept to others.

Chapter 1
Christian conscience

The pagan inheritance

Swiftly and seamlessly embraced by the early church, conscience is often thought to be Christian in its origins. But Latin *conscientia* was already a flourishing concept in Roman persuasive oratory and legal pleading well before the birth of Christ. Roman conscience gave texture and imagery to early Christian ideas of conscience, and many of its attributes would inform both Catholic and Protestant conceptions of conscience. Carried forward within these conceptions, it remains influential in views of conscience today.

The foundation of Classical conscience was public or social opinion. People at odds with public opinion or social consensus found themselves vulnerable to the accusations of conscience and to conscience's pangs. Cicero, in public address, enlisted and swayed opinion by weaving conscience into his arguments on behalf of clients and his denunciations of the guilty and proud. Conscience is, he says in *Pro Milo*, the principal theatre of virtue (*theatrum virtuti*), and one performs in that theatre for good or ill. His client Milo has come forward freely, he says, because the strength of conscience sustains him, even as it haunts those who have erred with visions of punishment. A good conscience, he suggests, can be a basis for legal acquittal. As for bad conscience, it joins legal sanction to punish those who have offended public standards. Forget about Furies, he says in *Pro Sexto Roscio*; the guilty torment themselves with the thought of their own evil deeds: each is harassed and maddened by the knowledge of his crime, terrified by his thoughts and his bad conscience. The forensic orator Quintilian argues that those who stray from the path of virtue suffer twice over, from the penalties of the law and, invariably, those of bad conscience (*semper vero malae conscientiae*). In his 1st-century BC *Civil Wars*, Julius Caesar tells of corrupt officers who suffer the opprobrium of their familiars, and also internally in conscience of mind or spirit (*animi conscientia*). And Cicero again, speaking of Caesar in his *De Officiis*, exclaims, 'What stains of conscience [*conscientiae labes*] do you suppose he had, what wounds to his spirit?' So familiar are conscience's traits that a contemporary rhetorical handbook, *Rhetorica ad Herennium*, advises the prosecutor to say that his adversary has displayed the signs of conscience, or *signa conscientiae*: that he was seen to have blushed, grown pale, stammered, spoken inconsistently, displayed uncertainty, compromised himself.

This language of conscience – including its capacity to cajole, to wound, to mark or stain – has a familiar ring to it, for conscience is already up to its 2,000-year endeavour of harassing the bad and upholding the good, and visiting pain, terror, pallor, and trepidation upon those who ignore its strictures. This language and imagery were well suited to the emergent Christian religion, faced with multiple tasks of converting the hesitant, disciplining new believers, and encouraging self-vigilance and personal reform within its ranks. Already proven as a spur to action and an incentive to life-change, conscience was conveniently adaptable to Christian aspirations and needs. No wonder it was embraced and elaborated with such zest that it became an early and crucial component of the Christian worldview.

Catholicism and conscience

The crucial event for the Christian appropriation of conscience was Jerome's choice of the Latin *conscientia* in his late 4th-century translation of the New Testament from Greek to Latin. In the Greek testament, Paul's Epistles rely upon the term *syneidesis*, a broadly inclusive term which anticipates *conscientia* in its suggestion of mutual knowing, or a knowing by the self 'that knows with itself'. By translating the noun *syneidesis* as *conscientia*, Jerome introduced it at one stroke as a crucial category of Christian self-understanding. The two terms are not, of course, precisely equivalent. In choosing *conscientia*, Jerome could not avoid certain of its previously formed connotations. For one thing, the pre-history of *conscientia* connected it inevitably to public expectation and the public sphere. While *syneidesis* was an inner quality, inherent in the individual, *conscientia* was a term that looked, Janus-faced, in two directions: inwardly, to be sure, but also outwardly, as in Ciceronian and Classical-legal understanding, to public opinion and shared values. The character of biblical and Christian conscience was thus mixed at its very inception, combining principles of private ethical discernment with public expectation. This fusion – or one might say potential confusion – of the internal and the external forums meant that Christian conscience would always potentially serve two masters: its possessor or subject, on the one hand, and the doctrinal or theological views of its ecclesiastical sponsor, on the other.

The formulations of conscience in Paul's Epistles, as carried forward to the West in Jerome's Latin translation, would remain as touchstones, and also as occasions of debate, throughout subsequent Christian history. The most influential of all occurs in Romans 2:14–16, in which Paul explains that the Jews are governed by their laws, but that Gentiles or Christians are a law unto themselves, and show the work of the law written in their hearts, their conscience rendering testimony to them (*ostendunt opus legis scriptum in cordibus suis testimonium reddente illis conscientia ipsorum).* Paul's conscience is thus very intimate to the individual who possesses it; a direct and personal gift from God to the believer – a view that would become increasingly important to the rise of various early modern protestantisms. Yet his conscience also plays a more public and judicial role, adjudicating between various thoughts and, finally, testifying before God at the Day of Judgement.

Crucial elements of the late Christian conscience are already on view in St Augustine of Hippo's late–4th-century account of his conversion to the Christian religion. Augustine was born a pagan, trained in classical literature and philosophy, and flirted with various systems of belief before converting to Christianity and assuming his mandate as one of the Fathers of the Roman Church. In his 397–8 *Confessions*, he describes his path to Christian conversion, a path involving a good deal of diversion and delay. Even after a number of his friends have converted, he hesitates, awaiting certainty about his choice. In this state, he is addressed by his own conscience, a conscience already aroused over his unnecessary delay:

> The day had come when I should be naked to myself and my conscience [*conscientia mea*] mutter within me: 'Where is my tongue? Indeed you kept saying how that you would not cast off the burden of vanity for an uncertain truth. Behold, matters are now certain, and you are still burdened. And they are receiving wings on freer shoulders, others who have neither so worn themselves down in seeking nor spent ten years and more thinking about it.' Thus I was inwardly gnawed and violently confused with horrible shame.

Conscience speaks from a position shared with the self, but incorporates elements and perspectives external to the self. A decisive key to the ambivalence of conscience's location and behaviour rests in the etymology of the Latin word itself: as *con* + *scientia*; *scientia* as knowledge, but knowledge held *con*, or 'together with' or 'in common'. Conscience is knowledge of oneself, but also knowledge held together with another or others, or, reflexively, knowledge of oneself by oneself. Consequently, conscience appears to speak from within as interior knowledge – knowledge felt *intus*, or inwardly – but shows definite marks of a more expansive exterior knowledge as well. It is alert, for example, to what 'others' are doing and have done, to the fact that many of Augustine's associates have already converted.

Conscience's 'personality', marked by impatience and even a touch of irascibility, is already well formed. Although intimate with Augustine, it is hardly an enabler or abettor. It is a voice of 'loyal opposition', loyal but strenuous too. A subsequent sense of mutter or *increpare* is to 'chide', and Augustine's conscience does plenty of that. Assailing Augustine for his spiritual prevarication, it displays an ability to 'gnaw' at him and to stir *pudor*, or shame – attributes of conscience which persist to this day. Its arsenal of characteristic devices includes not only incessant nagging, but also cruel parody of Augustine's own hesitations and rationalizations. The best we can say for conscience is that its impetus is affirmative, and bent on self-improvement. Its voice is action-seeking, and it will not fall silent until it has achieved its goals.

Why does Augustine tolerate this finicky and ultimately implacable co-presence? In part because it is already there, already inside the gates of the self, and must in any case be reckoned with. And also in part because it bears special knowledge and authority, of a broader sort; superior knowledge that must be taken into account. To put it differently: conscience knows everything Augustine knows (everything about his ten years of prevarication and delay) and also knows more besides (everything about the superior character of Christian knowledge and the better use Augustine's friends have been making of their time). Taking full advantage of this superior strategic location – at the boundary of the self and the other – conscience is well suited to hail Augustine into a new stage of awareness about himself and the choices he has been making in the world.

In this protean form, early Christian conscience was bequeathed to subsequent generations, in the period we now call the Middle Ages, when, under the sponsorship of the Church, it both flourished and elaborated some of its most productive inconsistencies. As a voice straddling the inner and the outer, it is alternately friend and foe, at some times supportively encouraging and at other times harshly corrective. It knows one's worst foibles, but it addresses them within broadly entertained and rationally accessible norms. It simultaneously institutes a strengthened sense of selfhood, on the one hand, and a permanent division of that self between private inclination and public consensus, on the other. Already mixed – and in this sense both vital and unstable – at its point of inception, Christian conscience was thus guaranteed a long subsequent history of enormous influence and endless doctrinal contention.

In one respect, however, the union of Church and conscience in the medieval period had a stabilizing effect. For the first time, rather than shifting with the tides of situation and public opinion, conscience was furnished with a secure body of content in the form of Christian theology, biblical precedent, and institutional practice. Medieval conscience retains its capacity to speak within, and to address the inner person, but need not in most cases wonder about what to say.

This state of affairs, in which conscience 'arrives' already bearing information about right conduct and belief, is captured in one of the fuller medieval treatments of the subject, Benedictine monk Peter of Celle's *On Conscience*. There, a magnificent banquet hall is prepared, but the chief guest has not yet arrived:

> Imagine a table filled with a variety and abundance of different dishes ... Let everything be arranged in perfect order, so that nothing is wanting in elegance, nothing is superfluous or boring.

For the time being, however, let the most spacious and beautiful place, specially prepared for the queen and mistress of the house, remain empty... Finally there comes the woman at whose beauty the sun and moon are in awe, and as she sits down the doors are closed and the wedding feast has a full complement of guests. The mystical cases of scrolls... declare her name to the royal court: this lady is called 'Conscience'.

Dispatched by God to the receptive Christian soul, conscience does not come empty-handed. She bears cases of scrolls which not only contain her identity papers and charge, but also the contents of her well-stocked chamber. These contents, here and elsewhere, consist of views generally held and widely known: collective witness of saints and confessors, councils and synods, authorized commentary upon Latin scripture.

Similar observations may be made of the medieval English classics of conscience. The vivid title of *Ayenbite of Inwyt* (or 'Repeated Gnawing of Conscience') suggests a kind of self-generated guilt within, but the body of the text consists mainly in the enumeration of those external and consensual features of penance by which *all* Christians may regulate their lives: God's Commandments, the seven deadly sins and their branches, the rules of holy life, the *pater noster*, the cardinal virtues, the practice of shrift. Conscience, or *inwit*, arises only incidentally, as a by-product of good shrift, at which point the penitent will measure his own experience against the general tenets of the Church and will, in consequence, experience great sorrow, 'and often wet his bed with tears'. Despite the implication of its editorially assigned title, the 14th to 15th-century *Pricke of Conscience* is actually less an anatomy of an individual or singular conscience than a treatise on consensually known doctrine (the fear of death, hell, purgatory, the signs of judgement, the last things, and the rewards of heaven). Conscience is mentioned only incidentally in the poem, once as one of the fifteen accusers (along with devils, angels, martyrs, and so on) who will appear to testify against the wicked at the time of judgement, and once as one of the fourteen pains of hell (along with cold, hunger, and so on). Conscience will indeed, as always, cause individual and very particular discomfort – will 'gnaw' and 'bite as vermin' – but its contents are universally shared out and non-specific to the remorseful individual.

I certainly don't want to engage in sterile generalizations about the Middle Ages as a period of monolithic faith, because medieval conscience is itself a highly motile and flexible concept, and, even if the contours of its advice are generally predictable, all the familiar and conflicted issues of practical application remain. The depth and variety of medieval thinking about conscience may be illustrated in the case of a major 14th-century poem, William Langland's *Piers Plowman*. The poem is an allegory, in which the central character, Will, is a person faced, as his name would indicate, with difficult and challenging issues of discernment and choice. Many of the characters of the poem, including Conscience (the only character present throughout most of the books of the poem), represent attributes stationed both within and outside Will's mind. Conscience – now male, for he/she is a constant gender shifter – interacts with Will in a variety of ways, some too richly complex to be detailed here. His main responsibility is to sermonize Will, lecturing him about matters of doctrine that he should know and enact in his personal conduct. His advice thus consists mainly of common knowledge: things generally known, that every Christian should know, by which Will should guide his life and conduct. He is variously portrayed as keeper, counsellor, and guide, and Reason, his constant companion, abets and channels his enterprise.

Conscience, who earns a capital 'C' from some medieval scribes and all modern editors for his generalized character, cannot, however, be written off as two-dimensional. Part of his interest rests in his situation, both within and outside Will's mind. A voice in Will's head, he is also a serious player in the world. The official and public nature of his duties is emphasized in his various capacities and titles: he is a counsellor, guide, and holds office as constable of the castle of Unity. These worldly involvements lead him into repeated difficulty. Forced to make decisions in a compromised public sphere, he reveals fallibilities which might otherwise have gone unsuspected. He draws up a questionable guest list, including a pompous Doctor of Divinity, for a dinner party and finally needs to clear his head by walking out on his own guests; we see him besieged by external foes at the poem's end; and, despite warnings to the contrary, he makes the disastrous mistake of admitting Friars to the castle of Unity. The poem's ending suggests that he might be better off turning down some of his jobs, and making his way in a less institutional capacity, as wayfarer and pilgrim in the world. But, within the poem as we have it, Conscience has no choice but to grapple with flawed alternatives as he enacts his higher responsibility as an arbiter of Christian consensus.

Thus, in Langland's poem, Conscience stimulates constant issues of interpretation and application. But, even though Conscience may be temporarily bested, or may err in matters of particular choice, he never stumbles into outright doctrinal error, never defends deviant or idiosyncratic opinions formed outside the Church. Aquinas and other analysts would recognize the possibility of a heretical or erroneous conscience, but in most daily applications medieval conscience remains orthodox and well intentioned.

The familiar modern idea that conscience might stand alone, against every recognized authority, has yet to take full shape. Necessary to that shift is the conception of a private, internal conscience which may pit itself against a public or official Conscience. This shift is often associated with Martin Luther and the rise of Protestantism, yet its earliest signs may be found in the late medieval period, and even within the later versions of Langland's poem. *Piers Plowman* was composed in stages from the 1360s until the later 1380s, and its final version, known as the 'C' text, includes an insertion in which Will (now more closely associated than ever before with the authorial William Langland) is assigned a personal, as well as a general, conscience. More interestingly still, his personal conscience and his allegorical Conscience find themselves at debate. In this passage, Will is accused by Reason and Conscience of leading a spiritually dissolute or unproductive life. This occurs in a passage added to the beginning of the poem's fifth section, with Reason and Conscience challenging Will's layabout ways. Will replies (*to* Conscience!) that:

> . . . in my consience y knowe what Crist wolde [wishes] y wrouhte.
> Preyers of a parfit man and penaunce discret
> Is the leueste [most precious] labour that oure lord pleseth.

Conscience is unimpressed with Will's explanation that his personal conscience is compatible with his customary pursuits of offering prayers for wealthy patrons and performing penance now and then. In this passage, Conscience (as shared or collective entity) overrules Will's conscience (or personal sense of right and wrong) – but the very fact that institutional Conscience and personal conscience can fall into debate is tellingly predictive. Will's 'own' small-c conscience doesn't have anything terribly original to say; in fact, Conscience finds his remark obvious and superficial and angrily brushes it aside, and certainly Conscience prevails in the end. Nevertheless, this exchange between conscience and Conscience adumbrates a situation that would be more frequently seen in the 15th century and then become prevalent in the 16th century, in which a difference arises between an individual conscience and a more broadly held and institutionally supported view of Conscience. This difference might, in the late 14th-century version of *Piers Plowman*, be thought of as a kind of conceptual or potential space, an opening not yet filled by a really personal or ambitiously revisionary conscience, but within which such a personalized conscience might develop and thrive.

Will's appeal to personal conscience arises in a situation of duress, a situation in which he finds himself heavily pressed by Reason and Conscience. This is understandable. A character pressured by superior authority – and especially spiritual or religious authority – needs some kind of resort or fallback, and the resort to a personal conscience opens, at least, a small area of discretionary counter-argument. The 14th and 15th centuries in England, and also on the Continent, saw a multiplication of personal and doctrinal challenges to the institutional Church (some of which, like Langland's, sought modest revision of its practices, and others of which may be regarded as forebears of 16th-century Protestant disaffection). Individuals caught up in these challenges would find increasing solace in the idea of a personal rather than institutionally supervised conscience.

Although some orthodox writers of the 14th century, such as the vernacular theologian Walter Hilton and political factionalist Thomas Usk, appeal to concepts of personal conscience, the richest source of such appeals is to be found in the writings of theologian John Wyclif and his Lollard followers. These religious dissidents of the 14th and 15th centuries raised many issues that would be prominent in the 16th-century Protestant Reformation. Wyclif, pressed on every front by ecclesiastical authority on issues which would lead eventually to formal condemnation (and to the exhumation and burning of his body), argued in his Sermon 49 that individual Christians ought better to judge merit *in their own conscience* than relying upon the views of others, and went on to declare: the final forum of merit 'rests in my own conscience' ('*in consciencia mea propria stabilitur*'). His text for this sermon was, tellingly, and, in the light of subsequent history, predictively, from Galatians 6:5: 'each one will carry his own burden' ('*unusquisque onus suum portabit*').

But the first decades of the 16th century were the moment at which a newly individualized view of conscience became prominent in

England, and an opening wedge of this transformation may be found in the behaviour of two oddly matched adversaries.

Henry VIII and Chancellor More

To say that a *wholly* new view of conscience emerged in the 16th century would undervalue the subtlety and diversity of more than a millennium of previous consideration, and would underrate the unevenness with which such changes occur. Even so, marked new currents gain ascendance in the 16th century. Propelled by evangelical theology, with its emphasis on direct communication with God and the urgency of personal revelation, many people began to view conscience less as a matter of authoritative ecclesiastical consensus and more as a haven of singular, even idiosyncratic, opinion. In keeping with this new personalization, conscience came to be seen less as a body of ecclesiastical precepts imported from the 'outside in', and more as a set of deeply lodged convictions speaking from the 'inside out'. Rather than an ally of unity and unification of belief, conscience became a potentially divisive influence, an urgent, deeply interior prompting which might set one at odds with established institutions and patterns of belief, which might goad the person of conscience into situations of the utmost precariousness and danger, but must nevertheless be followed lest one risk the integrity and ultimate salvation of one's very soul.

The outlines of what may be considered a 'Reformation Conscience' are evident on the Continent by the early 1520s and in England soon after. The evangelical currents culminating in those movements popularly known as the Reformation are too complicated for simple description, but some of their features, as well as some elements of the Catholic response, may be viewed in the remarkable collision between Henry VIII and Sir Thomas (eventually Saint Thomas) More. Henry's adversary More has long been considered the primary exponent of conscience in his principled refusal to accept Henry's Supremacy Oath and

1. King Henry VIII: man of conscience? Portrait by Hans
Holbein the Younger, c. 1537

severance of ties with the Church of Rome, but Henry was himself
the surprising and persistent exponent of an even more radically
new form of personalized conscience.

In the spring and summer of 1527, Henry began his amorous dalliance with Anne Boleyn and began to gather his resolve to seek a divorce from Katherine, his longtime queen. His *grounds* were to be scriptural and legal-jurisdictional, bearing on the illegitimacy of his marriage to his brother's widow, but his *rationale* involved the torments of his *scrupulum conscienciae*, or scruple of conscience, a conscience responsible not to papal approval, or to conciliar authority, or the opinions of the public at large.

Earlier discussions of conscience undoubtedly occurred in closed session, but, as far as the written record goes, in December 1527 Wolsey explains to one of the king's emissaries, that:

> the King, partly by his assiduous study and learning, and partly by conference with theologians, has found his conscience somewhat burthened with his present marriage; and out of regard to the quiet of his soul, and next to the security of his succession . . . , he considers it would be offensive to God and man if he were to persist in it, and with great remorse of conscience has now for a long time felt that he is living under the offense of the Almighty.

Nor did Henry stray from this alibi; near the end of it all, in a letter of 16 April 1533, the emperor's envoy Chapuys, describing an interview in which Henry proved steadily obstinate and disclosed that he had already privately married Anne Boleyn, says that he begged Henry, no respecter of other men, at least to respect God: 'He told me that he did so, and that God and his conscience were on very good terms.'

Who can say whether Henry was *really* troubled in his conscience, or (as seems more likely) in some other part of his body. The point is that an emergent climate of opinion, which Henry clearly understood and grasped, allowed the exponent of a dubious or unpopular position to go a long way if he or she could lay persuasive claim to the promptings of a nagging personal conscience. Even if Henry's conscience-talk was all pretext, he was remarkably successful in wielding his influence as sovereign and his own argumentative skills to draw people into the discussion on terms which granted him a possible conscience claim. He got partial concessions, at least early on, even from staunch people like Cardinal John Fisher. In or around 1528, we find Fisher writing (nervously but hopefully), 'I am convinced that the royal wish is not at all to reject the laws of God. That, if on account of Levitical prohibitions, he has yielded to a scruple of conscience [*conscienciae scrupulum*] he will rightly set it aside.' The pope himself was rumoured to be considering a short-lived scheme by which Henry would have two wives, with the goal that Henry's conscience might be satisfied. So, too, do we find More, during his 1529–32 chancellorship, bending towards partial accommodation. More's own rather contorted position during his term of office was that he would assist the king in matters not *un*acceptable to his own conscience, but that persons other than himself might be enlisted to prosecute the great matter of the divorce, their number to include 'onely those (of whom his Grace had good nombre) whose conscience his Grace perceived well and fully persuaded vppon that parte'. More's early hope (which he would ruefully revise during the events of 1532–4) had been that Henry would find a way 'never...to put eny man in ruffle or trowble of his conscience' in this matter; that each participant's distinctive conscience would be sacrosanct. Thus we find even ultimate doubters like Fisher and More ready to bend at least part-way towards an emergent discourse about the sanctity of individual conscience.

Henry's own shift from a universally accessible conscience to an individualized one was accompanied by an ambitious ideological campaign. Early on, he enlisted and coached a battery of complicit theologians to compose the *Censurae*, a 1531 pamphlet of determinations favourable to his divorce. Their arguments advanced a theory of private conscience, or *privata conscientia*, resurrecting and greatly extending previously existing notions of the sanctity of a private law written in men's hearts.

Quoting from a nearly contemporaneous English translation of the original Latin:

> The public law is that, whiche hath ben confirmed by writynge of
> the holye fathers. The private lawe is the lawe that is written in
> mennes harts by the inspiration of the holye goste as thapostoll
> seaketh of certeyne, WHICHE have the lawe of god written in
> theyr hartes [*in corde hominum scribitur*].

In the concept of a private law written in men's hearts, we revisit that passage from Romans 2:14, a passage never, of course, forgotten, but which would gain newly prominent attention from a variety of evangelical and anti-institutional reformers. When one declares oneself moved by direct and personal communication with the Holy Ghost, and possessor of a law uniquely written on one's own heart, external tests in common law or the writings of the fathers or any other element of the Magisterium fall by the wayside:

> if we folowe the motion of the holy spirite and of our conscience we
> be not undeer the commune lawe whiche ever ouchte [*ought*] to give
> place to the pryvate lawe. For in tho thinges that be forbidden by
> the lawe of god we must obey our conscience: and in other thinges
> the churche.

The more traditional view of conscience, as chiding but non-renegade, obviously had more to offer to the embattled 16th-century Church of Rome than did the subjective and unruly *privata conscientia* favoured by Henry and his advisers. Cardinal Fisher would join the attack on private conscience in his 1531–2 *Apologia*. More, who had earlier bent part-way towards Henry's position in his expectation that individuals might be allowed to opt in or opt out of his programme, was forced finally by the Oath of Supremacy and Act of Succession to adopt a more resolutely traditional position. In his last letters of 1532–4, he took his stand against an errant individual conscience misdirected by an idiosyncratic or heretical individual against matters of common faith. Writing to his daughter Margaret, he spoke to this matter in the case of a man who would 'take away by hym self upon his owne minde alone, or with some fewe, or with never so many, against an evident trouthe appearing by the common faith of Christendome', finding that 'this conscience is very damnable'. In his later vicissitudes, More placed increasing emphasis on the idea of an external community of right belief. In the *Dialogue of Comfort*, for example, he recommends that the rule of conscience be submitted to external correction, if only in the limited form of advice from some other good man. In his last months in prison, most radically isolated and estranged from the advice of a good man or men, and more than usually pressured by circumstance to rely upon the promptings of his own conscience, he found a way to introduce a guardrail of external authority. This was to create his own inner voice or wise man and his own public or community. This community is un-present, drawn not from persons to whose conversation he enjoyed access but from what might be considered a 'moveable' body of synods, saints, and apostles, whose approval – and, if necessary, correction – he sought. He makes this point eloquently in his post-condemnation speech, as reported in Chastelman's *Memoirs*:

> The Chancellor interrupting him said, 'What, More, you wish to be considered wiser and of better conscience than all the bishops and nobles of the realm?' To this More replied, 'My lord, for one bishop of your opinion I have a hundred saints of mine; and for one parliament of yours, and God knows of what kind, I have all the General Councils for 1,000 years, and for one kingdom I have France and all the kingdoms of Christendom.'

A 'Reformation' conscience?

In the cases of Henry and More, we encounter contemporaries who hold the word 'conscience' in common but mean different things by it. Henry, More's successor Cromwell, and the mid-century

2. *Sir Thomas More Reflects*, by William Hickman Smith Aubrey, c. 1890

evangelicals surrounding Henry's son Edward VI laid unprecedented emphasis on the interiority, singularity, and the rigorousness of a personalized conscience's demands. Henry had reasons of his own to favour the inclinations of his *privata conscientia*, but more devout contemporaries and successors developed reliance upon private conscience into a new and rather ostentatious public identity. Does this identity express a distinctively 'Protestant' or 'Reformation' conscience? Probably so, and more so as this conscience was bolstered and supplemented by Continental example.

The strong current of specifically Protestant interest in conscience flowing England's way may be briefly epitomized in the writings of Martin Luther, with his unequivocal emphasis on *conscientia mea*. This emphasis is brought to particular focus in his celebrated 1521 declaration at Worms, pronouncing his conscience subject only to the words of God, and adding, 'I cannot nor will I retract anything, since it is never safe nor virtuous to go against conscience.' This idea that one might form a personal conclusion of conscience based solely upon access to the words of God available in scripture, and thus bypass Church authority altogether, could hardly go unmarked. No sooner, in fact, had he spoken than Johann Eck, secretary to the proceedings, cried out, in his own account of the matter: 'Lay aside your conscience, Martin! [*Depone conscientiam, Martine!*] you must lay it aside because it is in error.' Eck's quarrel was not, of course, with conscience as traditionally understood, but with a perniciously new sense of conscience as a highly personal and individual guide to conduct. Luther, confident that his position was already validated in scripture, had no intention of laying his conscience aside.

The quarrel was not simply with Bible-reading as such, but with Luther's insistence on his right to form his own conclusions about its recommendations. Luther avoided solipsism by accepting the text of scripture as his external 'control', but insisted on his own right to scriptural interpretation. What distressed the papal representatives was his refusal to grant intermediary authorities – the conclusions of councils and synods, for example – any role as arbiters of relations between the personal and the divine. Luther was announcing a new understanding of conscience, a shift from the institutionally bound conscience of Catholicism to what may indeed be considered a 'Reformation' conscience, bound only by its direct communication with God as revealed in scripture. This insistence on personal rather than institutional or collective scriptural interpretation meant that, from the point of view of the institution-minded representatives of the Roman Church, he was not really significantly bound at all. Thus, in his 1525 'On the Bondage of the Will', written as part of his quarrel with the Catholic humanist Erasmus, he insists that 'Consciences are bound only by a commandment of God, so that the interfering tyranny of the popes . . . has simply no place in our midst.' The crucial thing for Luther was that the direct infusion of the Holy Spirit is freeing, rather than directing, whereas Erasmus's deference to institutions, whether ecclesiastical or political, can only be understood to bind and restrict: 'Human statutes cannot be observed together with the Word of God, because they bind consciences, while the Word sets them free.'

Protestant claims upon conscience did not, of course, diminish the loyalty of Catholics to their own understanding of the same ideal. But what might be called 'Catholic' and 'Protestant' views began to diverge. Both Catholic Erasmus and Protestant Luther claimed the warrant of 'conscience' for their reading of scripture and hence as their compass in life. But Luther mounts the typical Evangelical claim that *mea conscientia*, or personal conscience, is the basis for his interpretation of the Bible, whereas Erasmus makes a characteristically temperate claim that his interpretative practices are founded upon conscience and equally by the faculty of judgement. Erasmus (together with Aquinas and other giants of Catholic theology) thinks of conscience as closely linked with *synderesis*, an inborn faculty of rational choice among competing alternatives. Luther thinks no such thing; his conscience has the character of a lightning-bolt, a searing and life-transforming and utterly singular message from the Holy Spirit, and one which (so clearly in Calvin) the human subject can barely sustain. 'The Holy Spirit', Luther announces, *contra* Erasmus, 'is no Skeptic, and it is not doubts or mere opinions that he has written on our hearts, but assertions more sure and certain than life itself and all experience.'

3. Martin Luther at Worms

Newfound doubts

Yet Reformation conscience ran into doubts and difficulties at its very moment of apparent triumph. The emancipation of Evangelical conscience from constraints of dogma and consensual belief was certainly triumphal in its overtones. (Triumphal overtones are evident in contemporary images of Luther leading a newly emancipated conscience from the ruins of the Popish synagogue.) No sooner was the idea of an autonomous and indwelling and potentially infallible conscience consolidated than it fell prey to a host of doubts and perceived inadequacies. This interior and personal conscience suddenly seemed to many of its strongest partisans potentially fallible, and only doubtfully adequate to the extreme responsibilities now imposed upon it. One set of challenges, more human than theological, revolves around the conscience's lonely entrapment within the body. The Reformation conscience, lingering longer and dwelling more deeply within, maintaining an inherently solitary vigil as it awaits new bulletins and instructions from the Holy Spirit, often found itself in the position of a lonely spy, parachuted into enemy territory with a shortwave radio and a dying battery, awaiting a message that might never come. Whatever else may be said of the institutionally based conscience of the Roman Church, it was never alone, never lacking in external props and supports, whether historical, institutional, or intrapersonal. Once freed of theological and conciliar restraint, and radically personalized in its operations, conscience itself became subject to a variety of cooptations and seductions; now indwelling, the property of the fallible individual to which it was allied, conscience fell under suspicion of self-delusion, insufficient resolution, and something akin to bodily corruption.

Newfound doubts about conscience do not escape Shakespeare's keen perception. *Hamlet* may practically be described as a play about the operations of conscience, and its portrayal is anything but encouraging. Claudius experiences the 'lash' of conscience but is unable to act upon it. Hamlet himself is finally paralysed, rather than energized by it. In his most famous soliloquy, poised between action and self-extinction, he hesitates over his dread of something after death,

> The undiscover'd country, from whose bourn
> No traveller returns, puzzles the will,
> And makes us rather bear those ills we have,

Than fly to others that we know not of?
Thus conscience doth make cowards of us all.
(3.1.78–82)

This disabling conscience is undoubtedly composed equally of the word's two early modern meanings: conscious*ness* (in the sense of uncomfortable awareness) and conscience (which troubles the mind with thoughts of after-life reprisals for sinful deeds). But either way, or both ways, conscience is here presented as deeply problematic, an impediment rather than a spur to action.

This view of suspect conscience is conspicuous within Shakespeare and Fletcher's *King Henry VIII (All is True)*, which uses the word 'conscience' 24 times, twice as often as any other work in the Shakespeare canon. *This* Henry's conscience becomes something of a body-part, imbued with desire for Anne Boleyn. Henry's conscience is 'tender'; he reflects upon the occasion when 'conscience first received a tenderness/ Scruple and prick' – not only a phallic pun but a reformulation of the medieval understanding in which conscience 'pricks' its guilty host, with conscience now seen as an organ capable of *being* pricked, as liable to its own corrupted kind of embodiment. Anne Boleyn's conscience is, in turn, described as vaginal in nature – 'soft cheverel conscience', made of pliant leather, which would 'stretch' to receive Henry's offerings.

The theology of the day can be equally racy in its description of this newly embodied conscience. Luther (in a passage cited by Edward Andrew) made imagistic mischief by comparing conscience to a woman's womb with the two testaments as testicles. At what might be considered the Reformation's Geneva epicentre, Calvin was having his own problems with conscience and embodiment. Whilst assigning a critical role to conscience, he viewed it less as a site of calm self-assessment and fair reckoning than as polluted ground wracked by agitation and stupefied by terror. In the course of his

Institutes, Calvin makes some familiar points about conscience as (in Thomas North's early translation) 'engraven of God in the myndes of men', and his conscience does familiar duty in disclosing sins before the judgement seat of God. Yet we also encounter new worries about whether this indwelling conscience is up to the tasks imposed upon it. For one thing, a wholly interior conscience, unreliant upon external or institutional supports, faces all the dangers of embodiment; of becoming overly partisan on behalf of its fallible host, and, worse yet, of 'going native' within its bodily home. Calvin imagines a physical conscience, a conscience displaying 'wounds'. Rather than goading its host to self-improvement, this conscience needs help in its own right, requires God as physician to 'heal its sore'. Hardly triumphal, this is a conscience at bay, shaken to the core, wholly intimidated by God's wrath: 'When oure conscience beholdeth onely indignation and vengeance, how canne it butte tremble and quake for fear?' This is a conscience that has lost, rather than gained, in self-confidence and in capacity to perform its admonitory duties. Only an 'euell conscience' would require such ministration, and its evil is deeply involved in the circumstances of its bodily sojourn. No longer a spark of reason, or a staunch friend, or even God's neutral account-keeper, Calvin's conscience itself quails before God's rightful suspicion.

Always, in Calvin and his followers, remains the far-end possibility of a conscience purified not by its own efforts but entirely by God's grace. The problem of a conscience left on its own to deal with the sinfulness of the world, or supported only by what Calvin regarded as the wholly insufficient mechanisms of penance, is that its exertions are inevitably insufficient in the face of the inexhaustibility of sin. In the third and final book of his *Institutes,* Calvin propounds a state of 'Christian liberty' in which the restraints of the Law, which can bring only trepidation to the Christian who measures his likely deserts before the bar of God, are supplanted by a visitation of the mercy of Christ. In this state of grace, conscience is regenerated and purified by Christ's mercy, freed from the encumbrances of Catholic sacramentalism and now found equal to all problems. Yet this state of certitude is liable to remain beyond the grasp of many ordinary Christians still struggling with problems of faith in the world.

A remarkable 16th-century English representative of the Calvinist conscience is Anne Vaughan Lock, who translated his sermons and wrote the first sonnet cycle in English. In her 'Meditation of a penitent sinner, upon the 51. Psalme', she shows a conscience both prostrate with personal incapacity, but still able to flay and wound. It is, on the one hand, stricken and abashed:

> The horror of my gilt doth dayly growe
> And growing weares my feble hope of grace.
> I fele and suffer in my thralled brest
> Secret remorse and gnawing of my hart.

Yet still, on the other hand, her conscience retains the capacity for over-reaction and violent reprisal:

> My cruell conscience with sharpned knife
> Doth splat my ripped hert, and layes abroade
> The lothesome secretes of my filthy life.

This penitential conscience is still entrapped somewhere short of the promise of Christian liberty, thrashing about in an alternation between timorous self-accusation and extreme over-reaction.

Luther and Calvin betray worries about the adequacy of conscience as a vessel for the expectations to be imposed upon it, but contemporaries emboldened – especially at second or third hand – by ideas about conscience as a warrant for radical upheaval could hardly be expected to grasp matters of nuance, or to be much hindered by Luther's warning that conscience must be bolstered at every point by scripture, or Calvin's warning that it awaits redemption by Christ's mercy and God's grace. In the hands of evangelical zealots, Luther's and Calvin's views could be bent to frightening consequences. Erasmus, writing to Luther a year before the 1525 onset of the Peasants' War, warned of tumult to come: 'I see friendships torn asunder and I fear lest a bloody tumult should arise.' To this, Luther scornfully replied that the Word of God is *supposed* to issue in tumult, citing Matthew 10:34, 'I have come not to bring peace but a sword'. Faced with the actual disturbances of 1525, Luther was emphatic in his disavowals and his expectation of their suppression by the civil arm. Even so, as with other kinds of intemperate utterance, Luther had no final authority over how his words would be understood, and there were genuine social radicals, as well as religious zealots, out there. The insurrectionary Anabaptist Thomas Müntzer, a leader of the 1525 Peasants' War who held that true believers are animated by the Spirit of God working within the heart, may, despite Luther's own strictures to the contrary, be thought something of a son of Luther. And, as Stephen Ozment has said, 'Applied to society, the theology of the heart becomes a truly revolutionary ideology.' From 15th-century Hussite risings in the Czechlands and 16th-century peasant wars in Central Europe through England's 17th-century Civil War, conscience and contending views of its dictates are found at the very heart of social upheaval.

No wonder that some nervous Protestants, like the Anglican Richard Hooker in his 1594 *Laws of Ecclesiastical Polity*, sought to reground or 'resolve' the conscience by re-containing it within institutional restraints. Hooker's particular concern is with those Puritans, Anabaptists, and members of related sects who prefer the fruits of 'special illumination' as manifested in reliance upon their 'own consciences' over against the judgements of councils and synods, seasoned bodies that provide an appropriate basis for belief. He refers to the traditional role of councils in the church, which was to weigh matters under dispute and to arrive at authoritative determinations, thus providing 'ground sufficient for any reasonable man's conscience to build the duty of obedience upon'. Hooker grants the apparent right of persons to resist laws which they believe in their hearts to be opposed to the law of God, but believes that such opposition must be abandoned when confronted by an argument which 'being proposed unto any man and understood, the mind cannot choose but inwardly assent'. Such arguments, he believes, are sufficient to discharge even the most sceptical conscience, since 'the public approbation given by the body of this whole church unto those things which are established, doth make it but probable that they are good'. This argument from collective authority is hardly new; it was a cornerstone of authority in the Roman Church, and was vigorously asserted, in England, in prosecutions of Wyclif and his followers in the 14th and 15th centuries. It is an argument to which the Anglican Hooker now returns, in response to conceptions of conscience which cloak opinion in what he describes as a 'mist of passionate affection'. Here he anticipates, and opposes, what 20th-century Catholic philosopher Max Scheler describes as the 'principle of moral anarchy' which arises when 'anyone can ... appeal to his "conscience" and demand absolute recognition of what he says from others'.

Some continuing Christian perspectives

Conscience has both spiritual and ethical dimensions, and it has survived as a secular ethical principle without the support of religious belief. But spiritually based theories of conscience remain an active force in the world today, since religion is often tacitly or implicitly present even in many apparently secular belief systems. Spiritually based conceptions of conscience today confront a familiar definitional problem: balancing claims of singular, interior revelation with general, institutional authority.

In his 1913–16 *Formalism in Ethics*, Max Scheler searches for a mean between highly personal conscience, on the one hand, and universalism, on the other. He trenchantly argues that, indeed, conscience correctly holds a brief for that which is 'good for *you*, and *you alone*', but that the claims of an individual conscience must also be advanced within a more general commitment to moral insight:

> Only the cooperation of conscience and principles of authority and the contents of tradition with the mutual correction of… subjective sources of cognition guarantees [this insight].

His point is that the solitary conscience, or the claim of a uniquely illuminated conscience, courts ethical chaos, unless authority and tradition are accorded a tempering role.

Scheler was a Catholic theologian, and recognizably so, but occupies what may be a minority position in the contemporary Catholic Church. A more stringently authoritarian Catholic tradition may be found in the writings of Cardinal Ratzinger, now Pope Benedict XVI, who surveys the possible varieties of ethical relativism and comes down hard on the side of institutional authority, not just as one element of a poised view, but as a matter of final determination. In his 'Conscience and Truth' (1991), Ratzinger curtails the role of conscience in several respects. He argues, reasonably enough, that a purely subjective conscience can err. But he then proposes, less persuasively, that a conscience-based sense of guilt is a specious and unnecessary form of consciousness that needs to be addressed outside the arena of personal ethical choice. All men, in his view, possess a previously implanted love of Truth and the Good, but this faculty is at times forgotten and humankind cannot be expected to recover it unaided. The role of Catholic authority is to assist errant and forgetful man in the rediscovery of this hidden capacity. Conscience, in short, needs authority in order to hear itself or to discern its right objects. Conscience is, in this sense, a second-order phenomenon, and guilt over one's misdeeds is a second-order and imaginary emotion; the role of ecclesiastical authority is to reacquaint conscience with prior Truth, even as guilt can be more properly extirpated through the Atonement of Christ.

Returning for a moment to Scheler's triad of conscience, authority, and tradition, I suggest that Ratzinger overvalues authority and undervalues conscience, with the effect of diminishing the injunction to individual responsibility in ethical choice. (By an odd coincidence, he here partially parallels Calvin's previous argument that unaided conscience, and the throes of conscience-derived guilt, will be unequal to their tasks unless redeemed by God's grace.) The contrary argument can be made that a proper Christian conscience needs to act in conjunction with some sense of personal guilt as a condition of its effective operation. In an essay in *Morality and Beyond*, liberal Protestant theologian Paul Tillich remains true to earlier Reformation traditions by arguing that personal guilt is in fact conscience's default condition. He argues (in a vein informed by Nietszche but drawing a different conclusion) that 'the uneasy, accusing, and judging conscience is the original phenomenon; that good conscience is only the absence of bad conscience...'. The 'ego-self and conscience', he argues, 'grow in mutual dependence, and...the self discovers itself in the experience of a split between what it is and what it ought to be', with guilt as the symptom of this split. Tillich, however, is a basically optimistic thinker; rather than succumbing to its own trepidations, his guilty conscience is put to constructive work as an affirmative incentive towards self-reformation.

I don't have a Protestant pope to cite on these matters, but the sway of liberal theologians Paul Tillich and Reinhold Niebuhr in the mid-20th century might come as close as possible to a moment when an educated Protestant consensus about the self and the uses of conscience can be glimpsed. Revising Scheler's 'tradition' in the direction of something like 'enlightened social consensus', these theologians propose the social character of existence and the rightful claim of general social welfare to delimit individual excess as the positive values towards which a restless conscience might gravitate. Tillich urges upon subjects of conscience 'a movement of self-judgment and self-guidance which cannot come to rest until it makes its reference to a universal other and a universal community' – and that in the universal aspiration may be discerned, at least weakly, the presence of God.

Such communitarian positions are liable to be found flabby and relativist by modern-day evangelicals, who suspect liberal Protestantism's communitarian social gospel and faith in communal good will. In fact, Niebuhr himself entertained a parallel worry, which he expressed as a concern with modern man's persistent satisfaction in his own 'good conscience'. In *The Nature and Destiny of Man* (1941), he looked about himself, noting this 'universality of easy conscience among moderns', and marvelled that:

> Contemporary history is filled with manifestations of man's hysterias and furies; with evidences of his daemonic capacity and inclination to break the harmonies of nature and defy the prudent canons of rational restraint. Yet no culmination of contradictory evidence seems to disturb modern man's good opinion of himself.

The extremities of the Holocaust, and other ethical cataclysms since Niebuhr wrote in 1941, have undoubtedly undermined some of the complacency of which he spoke. Yet liberal Protestant theology does lie open to accusations of over-deference and social accommodation. Surveys reveal that the material of most sermons in the traditional Protestant churches of today concerns social adjustment and self-help rather than spiritual issues of errancy and salvation, and, from the views of the Reverend Butler in the 18th century through to the established denominations of today, conscience might be accused of a certain 'watering down', with respect to its responsibility for driving the errant sinner to repentance and salvation.

The idea of a personal, and implacable, conscience still holds sway in contemporary evangelical precincts, unchecked either by authority or tradition. No less than in the late 17th century, when

John Locke denounced unregulated enthusiasm, the evangelical true believer responds to a light in his or her own mind, thinking it from God, even if it is in fact 'nothing but the strength of his own persuasion'. Overheated and underauthorized consciences retain their capacity to stimulate abrupt action in the world, and the continuing personal conviction of divine mandate magnifies their effect, for good or ill.

Perhaps since its inception, and certainly now, 'Christian conscience' is a highly pluralized, rather than singular, phenomenon. Yet its varied Catholic and Protestant realizations retain considerable – if no longer exclusive – force in the world today.

Chapter 2
The secularization
of conscience

The emancipation of conscience from institutional religion is normally viewed as a consequence of Enlightenment secularization. But it may also be viewed, rather more paradoxically, as an unintended consequence of 16th- and 17th-century evangelical fervour. Calvin's attacks on conscience were unrelenting. He portrayed it, on the one hand, as a severe critic certain to find humankind unworthy of salvation and, on the other hand, as a chastened and timorous faculty, insufficient to its task and quailing before God. The effect of Calvin's theology was not only to bypass the confessional and penitential structures of the institutional church, but also to bypass conscience as an effective agent of salvation, preferring instead to make salvation a matter to be determined by the character of the individual's faith in Christ. In evangelical Protestantism, conscience was thus effectively deinstitutionalized, wrenched from its moorings as an ecclesiastically approved incentive to self-reformation and good works. It was left as a kind of desperate freelancer or improvisatory actor, alternately ingratiating itself with and terrorized by God, sometimes lashing out at its host and at other times abjectly confessing its own insufficiency.

The special relationship between conscience and organized religious belief was not, of course, to end altogether. Not only does conscience still enjoy considerable support within organized

Christian denominations, but God remains an implicit or shadowed presence as a sponsor or guarantor within many apparently secular systems of contemporary belief. Even today, many occasions of conscience in which God is not directly invoked may still be found, upon examination, to pivot or depend upon divine authorization as an absent cause or ultimate sanction. Still, although God may hover somewhere in the wings of the modern theatre of conscience, divine involvement tends increasingly to be treated as a kind of 'last instance', a formal acknowledgement which, like other kinds of logical last instance, never actually arrives.

A loosening of the ties between religious observance and individual conscience created a situation hospitable to the emergence of a more 'worldly' conscience. Or one might actually say 're-emergence': after all, Roman *conscientia* was social rather than religious in its inception, and so a precedent for a view of conscience either partially or even wholly independent of religious sanction was always at hand. From the late 17th century, an effectively secular conscience would vie with its more explicitly Christian counterparts for influence in the regulation of human affairs.

But, if conscience is to operate without the support and arbitration of an institutional church and without a secure status as a deputy of God, it risks devolution into the status of meddling busybody, a tattletale or arbitrary scold. Necessary to the perpetuation of a secular conscience is a conceptual regrounding, a broadened re-authorization for its operations in the world. This re-authorizing task proceeded at various cultural levels, and with various degrees of rigour, but a significant amount of explanatory heavy lifting fell to a succession of remarkable Enlightenment philosophers, essayists, and divines.

Conscience un-churched

The liberation of conscience from the supervision of this or that religious denomination received an early impetus from 17th-century discussions of broadened toleration for a variety of religious beliefs. Such discussions were normally quite theistic, as was, for example, John Milton's 'Treatise of Civil Power in Ecclesiastical Causes', but such arguments for freedom in matters of religious choice and religious belief created a favourable ground for expanded intellectual freedom of all kinds, including increased freedom of conscience.

A significant broadening of the discussion in the direction of intellectual freedom occurs in the writings of John Locke, beginning with his *Letter Concerning Toleration* (1689). Because his argument in this tract originates in concern over intolerance among different sections of the Christian religion, it can hardly be thought an irreligious or non-religious text. Nevertheless, it introduces an enlarged perspective by grounding its argument for liberty of religious conscience upon a concept of natural rights. Locke's proposal is that sectarian jealousies, of which England had recently experienced so many with such dire consequences, would abate, if only 'Churches were obliged to lay down toleration as the foundation of their own liberty, and teach that liberty of conscience is every man's natural right, equally belonging to dissenters as to themselves.' Although religious conflict is his subject, he does not restrict his conclusions to that sphere. He argues, instead, that various conclusions of conscience should be treated as natural and inviolable, by civil authority as well as by the religious authority of an established or dominant church. Religious exercise remains a special domain of conscience, but civil law is allowed its rights and responsibilities in the matter. Boundaries between religious exercise and state oversight are blurred, since an individual Christian who feels prompted by religious conviction to violate a civil law remains liable to civil penalty and should accept that penalty as the consequence of his choice or action. God is still somewhere in this mix, but civil law has begun to assume authority in its own right, dictating rules of tolerance and reasonable conduct. As envisioned in the *Letter Concerning Toleration*, this mixed conscience cannot precisely be described as 'secular' in its operations. Nevertheless, Locke creates a *structure* for the proper exercise of conscience within a community governed by civil law; a structure that allows for a view of conscience as divinely prompted, but does not insist upon such promptings in order to be recognized as conscience.

In his *Essay Concerning Human Understanding* (1690), he returns to similar issues in a more secular argumentative frame, and presumes a different form of regulation for conscience – that it be governed by the elevation and exercise of human reason. He rejects unexamined claims that conscience proceeds from innate conviction (that one was born with it) or a gift of divine inspiration (that God put it there). Instead, reason is the arbiter of its legitimacy, and reason, rather than a claim of divine inspiration, must determine the matter at hand. He does not deny the *possibility* of direct divine illumination, but contends that, if it fails to meet the test of reason, the claim of any such illumination is to be mistrusted. In any case, divine inspiration is not the primary source of moral rules. Rather, he argues:

> Many men may, by the same way they come to the knowledge of other things, come to assent to several moral rules, and be convinced of their obligations. Others also may come to be of the same mind, from their education, company, and customs of their country, which persuasions, however got, will serve to set conscience to work, *which is nothing else but our own opinion or judgement of the moral rectitude or pravity of our own actions.*

Disagreeing with Thomas Hobbes on most points, he would nevertheless agree that conscience is founded in 'opinion', and in consequence, conscience cannot be thought unified or inevitably authoritative in its demands. That this working conscience is partial and cultural, rather than definitive and innate, seems to him apparent from observation. He cites repeated examples, much in the tone and style of Michel de Montaigne, in which people expose babies, raise them for food, and the like, from which he concludes that 'if conscience be a proof of innate principles, contraries may be innate principles; since some men, with the same bent of conscience, prosecute what others avoid'. Again and again, he observes, we encounter 'enormities practised without remourse', suggesting that conscience is not, and cannot, be the same for all parties.

This is why he mistrusts those 'enthusiasts' who seek to impose upon others the conclusions of their own fierce or intolerant conviction. However persuaded the enthusiast may be that his views are the product of divine illumination, he is likely to find himself opposed by others of similar but divergent conviction:

> For if the light, which every one thinks he has in his mind, which in this case is nothing but the strength of his own persuasion, be an evidence that it is from God, contrary opinions have the same title to inspiration; and God will not only be the Father of lights, but of opposite and contradictory truths.

Any purported revelation, he concludes, must be evaluated upon some ground other than passionate conviction; must, in short, 'be judged of by reason'. Often, upon such examination, the opinions of the most persuaded may be discovered to have been 'founded neither on reason nor divine revelation, but rising from the conceits of a warmed or overweening brain ... '. Reason, a form of natural revelation, is the proper corrective to such overwarmed conceits, and its conclusions are to be preferred.

Locke personally experienced the Puritan–Anglican, Parliamentary–Monarchist conflicts of England in the 17th century – a series of conflicts in which extreme parties of fervent conviction laid equal claim to conscience as their guide. Disdaining unexamined claims of illumination and the sanctity of sheer conviction, he developed a view of conscience which, although urbane on the question of whether or not divine sanction *might* be adduced in its favour, in no way *depends* upon divine sanction for its exercise or its ultimate evaluation. After Locke, a view of conscience may or may not claim divine authorization, but it certainly need not base its case for ethical attention upon any such claim. For the first time since the Romans, conscience is back in the world, and its principal supports are custom, consensus, and the exercise of reason.

There's a loss and a gain here. The loss is that, in detaching conscience from divine revelation and rendering it partial, situational, and subject to the test of reason, Locke diminishes its unquestioned authority. But the gain lies in the establishment of conscience as a limited but influential meaning-making system in a wider range of human affairs. This is a demystified and decentred conscience, a conscience stripped of its mantle of spurious infallibility, but a conscience prepared to enter as a robust contestant in the arena of worldly conduct.

Following Locke in some respects was Anthony Ashley-Cooper, the Third Earl of Shaftesbury, who believed that people possess an innate 'moral sense', even as he viewed that sense as open to judgement and correction by reason. In his 1711–14 *Characteristicks of Men, Matters, Opinions, Times*, he developed a concept of 'natural affection' supported by self-examination as foundational to human conduct. Shaftesbury assigns responsibility for such examination to conscience, a faculty which identifies ill-deserving conduct, and is to be distinguished from simple calculation of one's own interest. Conscience, so defined, is shared by all persons: even ill-doers, in his view, recognize that they deserve ill in return. Conscience may, he observes rather impartially, be understood in either a moral or a religious sense, but he finds that religious conscience relies upon moral or natural conscience, which are thus indispensable to its operation. Because we have reason to fear God's punishment only when we already know that we have committed a blameworthy act, our estimation of our actions thus has priority over any fears we might entertain about divine wrath. In other words, the determination of blameworthy conduct is our own, and subjective, and based upon criteria of natural assessment. God is presented as a spectator of our own process of self-assessment; as a 'suppos'd Being' to whom natural veneration is due, but not as a consequential actor within the process:

> [Conscience] has its force however from the apprehended moral Deformity and Odiousness of any Act, with respect purely to the Divine Presence, and the natural Veneration due to such a suppos'd Being. For in such a preference, the Shame of Villany or Vice must have its force, independently of that further Apprehension of such a Being, and his Dispensation of particular Rewards or Punishments in a future State.

Although Shaftesbury speaks with a good deal of apparent respect of this being, he also takes pains to exclude him from any significant role; our final determination of our own actions is achieved 'independently' of God's magisterial capacities for reward or punishment. Religion can, in fact, have a deformative effect in Shaftesbury's system, as when we commit an ill-deserving act as a result of 'any suppos'd Injunction or Command of higher Powers'. Such powers, he affirms additionally, are simply unnecessary, either to the instigation or the evaluation of an act; even, he says, 'excluding for ever all Thoughts and Suspicions of any superior Powers', the guilty will still be punished in their own opinions, even if only in the secondary or derivative sense of having compromised their own interest or happiness. Though arrayed in the terminology of a kind of attenuated theism, his is a worldly and effectively secular conscience – evaluated within social interaction and based upon a concept of personal shame.

Shaftesbury was, in turn, a major influence upon Joseph Butler, a divine who addressed matters of conscience in his 1726 *Fifteen Sermons Preached at the Rolls Chapel*. Although his reputation has receded, he may be considered the most popular spokesperson on matters of conscience in 18th-century England, and his views have certainly been absorbed within popular views of conscience persisting in the 19th century and operative today. He piously grants that conscience is a gift of God – a faculty 'placed within by our proper governor' and 'assigned to us by the Author of our nature' – but this gift, once given, appears to have no further reliance upon God for its continuing operation. Butler's conscience is a form of 'Reflection . . . , an Approbation of some Principles or Actions, and Disapprobation of others'. This conscience resides in our nature, and its undistorted or proper functioning should allow anyone to choose 'Humanity over Cruelty' as a matter of course.

In a telling shift from earlier evangelical theologies, which treated conscience as the Law of God written in men's hearts, Butler finds a variety of dispositions, some for good and some for ill, written in our hearts, and he situates conscience as that faculty which, serving as 'witness' of our dispositions, allows us to discriminate among them. The judgements of our conscience are, in his view, eligible to be 'seconded and affirmed' by God, but he assigns God a merely technical or initiatory role, together with (as in Shaftesbury) such additional influence as our natural desire to merit God's good opinion would inspire. Further restricting the avenues of God's influence upon our moral or ethical decisions, Butler opposes any 'tyranny' of established religion over conscience. Although believing a religious establishment necessary to the constitution of civil government, he echoes Locke by pleading for religious tolerance and non-interference in matters of conscience:

> A religious establishment without a toleration of such as think they cannot in conscience conform to it, is itself a general tyranny; because it claims absolute authority over conscience: and would soon beget particular kinds of tyranny of the worse sort.

Butler might be seen to reiterate – but in an utterly different tonality – Calvin's mistrust of the dominion of organized religion over individual choice. Not only, though, does he criticize the coercive power of the church, but he proceeds to a position that would have dismayed earlier evangelical Protestants by restricting God's access to the individual Christian's heart, and thus founding choice on reason rather than inspiration. Butler holds that we express our reverence to God through exercise of our powers of rational choice, an effectively Deist position that no evangelical would have recognized as religion at all.

Conscience and social consensus

The most influential 18th-century philosophers placed increasing emphasis on concepts of reason, affection, and, ultimately, feeling in matters of ethical choice. Yet any process of ethical choice which occurs entirely within the mind of the agent remains vulnerable to circularity and possible fallacy. Reason alone, or even reason applied to empirical evidence, is insufficient to oversee the operations of conscience; especially when applied by the solitary individual, reason remains vulnerable to error or to interest, when exercised in the absence of outside authority or constraint. If the constraint is not to be provided by an actively interventionist God, or by the dictates of religion – and neither Locke nor Shaftesbury thinks it should be – then a turn to social norms and consensus provides alternative grounding for a theory of moral conduct.

This is an idea which Immanuel Kant grasped with economical concision in his *Metaphysics of Morals* (1797). In his view, conscience conducts an 'internal court in man', addressing him in a voice that even the depraved cannot help but hear. This is the voice of a predisposition to judgement, incorporated in one's very being; but the problem with this voice, and with a wholly internal court, is that one cannot objectively judge oneself; cannot, without conflict of interest, fuse the roles of prosecutor, jury, and final judge. Given the difficulty of assessing one's own behaviour, one must stipulate a vantage from somewhere outside the ambit of personal choice, from which that choice can be assessed. Kant's proposed solution is to argue that, even though the business of conscience is that of a man with himself, its conclusions must be considered as if they were those of another person:

> For all duties of a man's conscience will, accordingly, have to think of *someone other* than himself ... as the judge of his action, if conscience is not to be in contradiction with itself.

This 'other person' may, in Kant's formulation, be actual or a merely ideal person that reason creates for itself. Its ultimate embodiment is God, but God as a subjective principle rather than an entity in its own right:

> Such an ideal person (the authorized judge of conscience) must be a scrutinizer of hearts, since the court is set up *within* the human being. But he must also *impose all obligation*, that is, he must be, or be thought as, a person in relation to whom all duties whatsoever are to be regarded as his commands. ... Since such an omnipotent moral being is called God, conscience must be thought of as the subjective principle of being accountable to God for all one's deeds.

Yet, he emphasizes, this is our principle, we construct it ourselves: 'In fact the latter concept is always contained ... in the moral self-awareness of conscience.' Although we labour internally to construct it, or Him, this judgemental concept finally draws upon materials external to ourselves; hence, it is a means by which social consensus and communally shared values flow back into the evaluation of a personal choice or act.

The person who most amiably puts all this on a social footing – a footing that need not deny God's involvement in matters of conscience but that by no means requires the presence of God – is the Scottish philosopher Adam Smith. Smith was Kant's slightly younger contemporary, and the precedent for Kant's view of

The 'court' of conscience

In England's Court of Chancery, also called Court of Conscience, all circumstances of a case could be considered with lessened legal formality. This linkage of court and conscience is suggestive. Whatever its shortcomings (read *Bleak House!*), the justice system at its best, like conscience at its best, seeks to balance rigour and mercy. Judicial metaphors have abounded throughout the history of conscience, employing concepts of advocacy, prosecution, jury determination, and final judgement to sharpen understanding of its procedures.

Roman conscience was intimately tied to judicial prosecution. In one of its earliest Christian appearances, conscience offers 'testimony' to our inner qualities (2 Corinthians 1:12). Calvin and the early Protestants imagine conscience as an implacable state's witness that apprehends the sinful and 'drags them forward as culprits to the bar of God'. Sir Thomas Browne moves the proceedings indoors, imagining 'a standing Court within us, examining, acquitting, and condemning at the tribunal of our selves'. Jonathan Swift extends the metaphor by arguing that conscience 'may properly be called both an accuser and a judge' – not, in fact, accuser alone, but a fearsome one, since 'whenever our conscience accuses us, we are certainly guilty'. Immanuel Kant also views conscience as a judge, but his worries lie in the opposite direction, fearing that self-interest may foster excessive lenience: 'to think of a human being who is accused by his conscience as one and the same person as the judge is an absurd way of representing a court, since then the prosecutor would always lose'. His solution is to re-level the playing field by challenging the person of conscience to think of 'someone other than himself as the judge of his actions'.

Conscience is like an independent judiciary; we can never be certain of its verdict, but it represents our best hope for a fair hearing and acquittal in the end.

conscience as impartial spectator is found in Smith's *Theory of Moral Sentiments* (1759), a work with which Kant was almost certainly acquainted. Smith is a boldly revisionary protagonist in any developing history of conscience, broadening its scope by regrounding it upon matters of moral judgement and articulating a system of conscience effectively independent of religious sanction. Smith does not utterly exclude the deity from his system, but introduces him in a weak form that allows him no independent sway in the judgement of human conduct. Sometimes, he concedes, even the impartial spectator, the 'demigod within the breast', is abashed by public disapproval of one's actions.

> In such cases, the only effectual consolation of humbled and afflicted man lies in an appeal to a still higher tribunal, to that of the all-seeing Judge of the world, whose eye can never be deceived.

The foundation of our belief in such a deity, however, requires further examination. Smith says that the idea of a world to come, when judgements will be set right by an unerring deity, is 'flattering to the grandeur of human nature' to an extent where we can hardly do without it. In other words, he doesn't precisely say, but implies, that this consolatory view of an unerring deity is a human invention. It is, in effect, a matter of priority, with man's ideas of human accountability preceding and informing his ideas of the divine:

> [man] must necessarily conceive himself as accountable to his fellow creatures, before he can form any idea of the Deity, or of the rules by which that Divine Being will judge of his conduct.

Smith anticipates Kant in the view that, 'We endeavour to examine our own conduct as we imagine any other fair and impartial spectator would examine it.' This act of reflective self-examination is not simply spun out of the person's own mind, but is in turn social: as Smith puts it, 'Man alone cannot reflect upon his behaviour.' It is, in consequence, not God or innate reason, but society and one's place in society that provides a norm for assessment: 'Bring him into society, and he is immediately provided with the mirror which he wanted before.' One's ethical being is dually comprised: by oneself and equally by oneself as another. In judging personal conduct, he says,

> I divide myself, as it were, into two persons; and ... I, the examiner and judge, represent a different character from that other I, the person whose conduct is examined and judged of. The first is the spectator, whose sentiments with regard to my own conduct I endeavour to enter into, by placing myself in his situation, and by considering how it would appear to me ... The second is the agent, the person whom I properly call myself, and of whose conduct, under the character of a spectator, I was endeavouring to form some opinion.

Objectivity is reintroduced by Smith's understanding that his second self speaks from a broader social platform, representing the enlarged perspective of a 'man of humanity in Europe', possessed of normative and uniform responses. Here we encounter a problem: that we of today doubt the existence of such a man, or, should such an ideally humane man exist, that his education, gender, and Western frame of reference necessarily qualify him as a final arbiter of all ethical situations arising in a heterogenous world. Smith's suggestion that we 'examine our own conduct as we imagine any other fair and impartial spectator would examine it' is attractive in its promise of self-scrutiny, but his 'impartial spectator' appears, upon examination, more and more an extension of Smith's own values, and less and less a fresh and irreproachably objective standpoint. To complete this critical litany, his untroubled assumptions about the ease of access to complete objectivity are unpersuasive from the standpoint of modern psychology or modern ethics.

Despite these objections, his endeavour – to look for a tempered norm both inside and outside oneself, and to correct individual disposition by the judgement of social consensus – remains highly laudable. Nor is his viewpoint cloying or soppy; his conscience can still scratch and bite and, like the awakened Furies of the *Oresteia*, drive an individual to self-reformation. Thus, even a person who commits a crime in secrecy will judge himself or herself adversely from the viewpoint of the impartial spectator: 'These natural pangs of an affrighted conscience are the daemons, the avenging furies, which, in this life, haunt the guilty.' For all Smith's sense of conscience as a matter of sympathetic intuition, he still delivers an admirable account of a conscience that aspires to self-correction; that is robust and interventionist; that concerns itself with matters of consequence.

The problem of public morality

The Enlightenment philosophers reject a narrowed conception of conscience and open its deliberations to larger horizons of social consensus. This enlarged perspective is essential to a robust conception of conscience, although it presents a new difficulty. By effectively severing the linkage between religion and conscience, and regrounding conscience within social consensus, Smith and others of his opinion risk leaving the conscientious individual at the mercy of uninterrogated public prejudice. With secular morality filling the void created by the diminishing role of God and religion in the sponsorship of conscience, the possibility arises that ethical choice might be engulfed by a tide of unquestioned external opinion. The very foundation of more modern respect for conscience has been its availability as an ally for the solitary individual at odds with established and coercive opinion, and so one can hardly be content with a view of conscience as a simple rendition of what 'everybody thinks'. The argument for rights of singular or even (with respect to prevailing views) deviant conscience in opposition to established forms and institutions of worship was memorably stated, and effectively carried, by Luther and other protagonists of the Protestant Reformation. But the subsequent argument, for the rights of individual conscience against settled opinion in a secular society, remains to be won.

This dilemma gains visibility in the 19th century, as views of conscience – some rigorous and others sentimental and popular – proliferate in civil society. The 19th-century novel seems at times a popular theatre of conscience, in which the concept is powerfully brought to bear as a mechanism for judging choices and actions in human society. As a socially situated form, the novel is particularly well suited to treat the particular problem of conscience in society, its tendency to ally itself with conventional morality.

Young Pip in *Great Expectations*, about to steal food and a file for the escaped Magwitch, has such a conscience – one which causes him a great deal of distress but is too blunted and conventional a tool to be of any use to him in the analysis of his predicament. Having first concealed a slice of bread down his trouser leg to fulfil his charge, he is violently assailed:

> Conscience is a dreadful thing when it accuses man or boy;
> but when, in the case of a boy, that secret burden co-operates with
> another secret burden down the leg of his trousers, it is (as I can
> testify) a great punishment.

On his way to discharge his errand, he finds himself accused by all nature, and slips into a hallucination:

> One black ox, with a white cravat on – who even had to my
> awakened conscience something of a clerical air – fixed me so
> obstinately with his eyes ... that I blubbered at him, 'I couldn't
> help it, sir. It wasn't for myself I took it!'

Pip would, obviously, be better off without so conventionalized a conscience at all; it is so deeply imbued with an uncritical and unreflective public morality that it hampers rather than advances his capacity to analyse the ambiguous situation in which he has been placed.

Later in the century, Twain's Huckleberry Finn gives us another victim of public morality and conventional conscience. Huck's complicity in Jim's escape from slavery would seem to give him less reason for self-accusation than Pip, who was arguably guilty of stealing family food for an apparent criminal, yet Huck indicts himself with a hodgepodge of conventional moralizations about theft and property-rights, good manners, and superficial religiosity. Here is Huck berating himself for allowing circumstance and his personal attachment to Jim to override public morality in aiding Jim's escape:

> ...who was to blame for it? Why, *me*. I couldn't get that out of my conscience, no how nor no way. It got to troubling me so I couldn't rest; I couldn't stay still in one place.... I tried to make out to myself that *I* warn't to blame, because *I* didn't run Jim off from his rightful owner; but it warn't no use, conscience up and says, every time, 'But you knowed he was running for his freedom'.... That was where it pinched. Conscience says to me, 'What had poor Miss Watson done to you, that you could see her nigger go off right under your eyes and never say one single word?'

4. Jiminy Cricket sporting a conscience badge ('Official Conscience')

The Talking Cricket

The 'Talking Cricket' of Collodi's 19th-century *Pinocchio* didn't fare well. He gave Pinocchio several pieces of beneficial advice before the irascible puppet squashed him against the wall with a wooden mallet. He rebounds, however, as 'Jiminy Cricket' in the 1940 Disney version, and is elevated by the Blue Fairy to the role of Pinocchio's conscience. She cites him as 'lord high keeper of the knowledge of right and wrong, counsellor in moments of high temptation, and guide along the straight and narrow path'. Jiminy first goes to work when the Blue Fairy tells Pinocchio that he must learn to choose between right and wrong. Pinocchio asks how he will know the difference, and she says his conscience will tell him. 'What are conscience?' he asks, suggesting that this faculty has yet to be activated, and at that point Jiminy appears: 'What are conscience! I'll tell ya! A conscience is that still small voice that people won't listen to.' Jiminy is becomingly modest about his capacities, enduring repeated setbacks and rebukes (Lampwick to Pinocchio: 'You mean to tell me you take orders from a grasshopper?'), but he perseveres and receives a gold conscience badge for his efforts.

Part of his perseverance might be ancestral. We first encounter this voice in the King James version, restraining Elijah for his excessive zeal: 'and after the fire *a still small voice*, And it was so, when Elijah heard it, that he wrapped his face in a mantle' (1 Kings 19:12–13). Protestant interpretative tradition has this as the voice of God, speaking as conscience. This prestigious background elevates Jiminy's stature. As does Gandhi's fondness for saying that 'The human voice can never reach the distance that is covered by the still small voice of conscience.'

Huck decides to turn Jim in, and writing a note disclosing Jim's whereabouts, he feels 'good and all washed clean of sin'. But, weighing the matter, he decides to tear up the paper, accepting the damnation that must accompany his unregenerate course. He concludes, '"All right, then, I'll *go* to hell" – and tore it up.' Huck employs the vocabulary of religious morality, but only in a misdirected sense. His case is a perfect illustration of Shaftesbury's point about the misapplication of religion to matters of conscience:

> to fear God any otherwise than as in consequence of some justly blamable and imputable Act, is to fear a *devilish* Nature, not a *divine* one. Nor does the Fear of Hell, or a thousand *Terrors* of the Deity imply Conscience.

A simulacrum of divine retribution is here confusedly introduced as enforcer of a misguided social norm. It is in fact the banality of public opinion, disguised as religion, that our two protagonists are unfurnished by their rather stunted consciences to resist. The cases of Pip and Huck demand that we seek a standpoint which comes to the aid of the individual prepared to challenge the prevailing values of the day, even when those values assume the guise of conscience itself. In each of these cases, and with more particularity in Huck's, a truer (if unnamed) and more inward conscience guides their actual choices, even in defiance of conventional or consensually held social views. This defiance might perhaps be described as 'ethical' and as issuing from an ethics of personal choice, rather than 'moral' and deriving from unexamined societal assumptions.

The situation of an embattled individual at odds with a petrified and stunted conscience reminds us that prevalent consensus is not necessarily a sufficient foundation for conscience; that a pressured conscience is anything but free; that to do the work for which we most respect it, conscience must operate independently of the narrow prejudice of

Gendering conscience

The protagonists arrayed in this volume inhabit something like a gentleman's club of conscience, an overwhelmingly male preserve. Sir Thomas More, imprisoned for his own scruple of conscience in refusing to sign the Oath of Succession, is unsurprised when his daughter Margaret tells him she has signed; comparing her amiably but devastatingly to the fallen temptress Eve, he supposes considerations of conscience irrelevant to her case.

Yet, recent centuries have seen an emancipation of female conscience, as women accept its blessings and burdens. Consider Brontë's *Jane Eyre*, in which Rochester and Jane each respond, and singularly, to its demands. Rochester possesses a rather traditional faculty that might be styled 'male' for its complacency and close affiliations with reason. At his first extended interview with Jane, he congratulates himself on his prominent frontal lobes, proclaiming 'I bear a conscience' while pointing 'to the prominences which are said to indicate that faculty'. He grants Jane a conscience, but still regards it as falling within his gift. In disguise as a fortune-teller, he interprets her own forehead, saying it announces her determination to follow 'the guiding of that still small voice ... ' But Jane's conscience has an emphatic presence of its own. 'Conscience', she says, resolving to leave Rochester despite her desire to remain, 'turned tyrant, held passion by the throat'. This conscience is fully voiced, and its voice is neither still nor small. It says to her, 'you shall tear yourself away, none shall help you; you shall, yourself, pluck out your right eye: yourself cut off your right hand'. And then, appearing arrayed in moonlight, as a shining female form, her conscience addresses her with an even more resolute intensity: 'My daughter, flee temptation!' To which Jane replies, 'Mother, I will.' Jane possesses a distinctive and active conscience, and it is gendered female.

prevailing opinion. These tenets are all persuasively argued by the utilitarian philosopher John Stuart Mill. Mill is perhaps more responsible than any other theorist of conscience for our contemporary sense of its mission to protect the minority from the majority, the unpopular but heartfelt position from the adverse weight of majority or predominate opinion. He demands tolerance, but moves well beyond previous arguments on its behalf. Mere religious tolerance, in the forms advocated by Locke, seems to him not nearly enough; in his view, tolerance must be extended to all varieties of political and social opinion. He equally opposes the tyranny of religious authority and the tyranny of state policy, declaring that 'whatever crushes individuality is despotism, by whatever name it may be called, and whether it professes to be enforcing the will of God or the injunctions of men'. His *Essay on Liberty* (1859) is explicitly concerned with 'the nature and limits of the power which can be legitimately exercised by society over the individual'. Individual autonomy and initiative can be bridled by external control only when individual interest collides with that of other people. Individual liberty, he argues:

> ...comprises, first, the inward domain of consciousness; demanding <u>liberty of conscience</u>, in the most comprehensive sense; liberty of thought and feeling; absolute freedom of opinion and sentiment on all subjects, practical or speculative, scientific, moral, or theological. The liberty of expressing and publishing opinions may seem to fall under a different principle, since it belongs to that part of the conduct of an individual which concerns other people; but, being almost of as much importance as the liberty of thought itself, and resting in great part on the same reasons, is practically inseparable from it. Secondly, the principle requires liberty of tastes and pursuits; of framing the plan of our life to suit our own character; of doing as we like, subject to such consequences as may follow; without impediment from our fellow-creatures, so long as what we

do does not harm them even though they should think our conduct foolish, perverse, or wrong.

Conscience, as Mill imagines it, is an aspect of 'consciousness'. Certainly, a free and untrammelled outlook is what he has in mind here, and not just a gnawing sense of duty, or any other of conscience's self-punishing attributes. He speaks directly to the dilemma experienced by Pip, Huck, and a range of other participants in Victorian society, in declaring his opposition to the varied forms of despotism, evident not only in religion and the state, but in the more pervasive tyranny of *collective opinion* and the *despotism of custom*. Mill argues, in effect, that the contents of an emancipated conscience are furnished neither by church nor state, nor collective opinion. Conscience is a matter for the singular individual, and those issues which Mill tackles with most vigour include support for dissenters from views upon which most persons are united, such as the necessity of belief in a God or an afterlife.

To these views his followers in the next century would add such matters as conscientious objection, the right not to follow one's own nation into war. Mill is, in short, a crucial initiator of the now-regnant view that conscience has a close connection with singularity and exception, and rights of conscience with the protection of fringe or minority opinion. In addition to his concern for the dissenting conscience, Mill would extend protection from belief to the arena of choice and action – to '*doing* as we like' – so long as no harm to others is done. (Here, he initiates a continuing discussion which will receive further consideration below, in Chapter 4.)

The tradition stretching from Locke through Mill, with its extension of rights and protections for individual conscience in secular as well as religious affairs, is one of the singular intellectual and ethical accomplishments of humankind. Despite the eloquence and persuasive power of such defenders, however,

5. John Stuart Mill

conscience also had its critics and detractors. Just at that mid-19th-century moment when Mill's writings signalled the consolidation of conscience as a bulwark of liberty and personal emancipation, conscience would be subjected to sustained, multiple, and influential attack by some of the writers and intellectuals most responsible for the shaping of 20th-century thought.

Chapter 3

Three critics of conscience: Dostoevsky, Nietzsche, Freud

During the 18th and 19th centuries, a number of religious thinkers like Butler and philosophical thinkers like Smith promulgated a hopeful view of an accessible and socially benevolent conscience. In their cultural dispersal, such views play out in Victorian commonplaces, like the sentimentalized moment captured in Holman Hunt's *The Awakening Conscience*. Hunt portrays a conscience-inspired illumination, in which a clever roué's seductive hopes are thwarted by a young woman's moral visitation. In Hunt's painting, and in a plethora of popular novels and fictionalizations, we see a confusion of conscience with something like public morality, in which, rather than underwriting a bold departure from ordinary expectation, conscience is the wedge by which community restraints and inhibitions impose themselves upon private behaviour. Yet the powerful engine of conscience is underworked, if harnessed only to the service of aligning personal behaviour with community values – the sorts of values we associate today with self-help books sold to busy travellers in airport news agencies. Fuzzily optimistic views of conscience as a reliable source of moral uplift could only annoy a range of more sceptical commentators.

The three critics of conscience I will discuss here are hardly a clique or cadre (although some lines of influence do unite them), but are united by their disdain for the idea of conscience as an

6. *The Awakening Conscience*, by William Holman Hunt, 1853

unproblematic agent of self-improvement or an unstinting advocate of public morality. The three pose an interrelated set of problems: what if conscience, rather than an authoritative voice of God, or enlightened social consensus, is a spurious and unnecessary burden? What if this is a burden we invent and unnecessarily impose upon ourselves? Or, worse still, what if we accept and internalize the dictates of overbearing or bogus external influences, thus yielding to a conscience comprised by ignorant prejudice and unexamined inhibition?

Conscience assailed

In Dostoevsky's *Crime and Punishment* (1866), the hero (or antihero) Raskolnikov dabbles early on with the idea that conscience – or, in this case, its close cousin 'instilled fear' – might actually represent an unnecessary restraint on human choice and action. He speculates that 'if man in fact is not a scoundrel...then the rest is all prejudice, instilled fear, and there are no barriers'. The rest of the novel devotes itself to showing that Raskolnikov is wrong, that barriers exist, but it does not leave these barriers unchallenged; it is searching in its examination of the mixed and often compromised legitimacy of these restraints we impose upon ourselves. Conscience, along with other sorts of scrupled unrest, is acknowledged as one of these barriers, and the grounds of its authority are subjected to constant and highly sceptical examination.

Raskolnikov presses his case against conscience in a controversial article in which he claims that 'an "extraordinary" man has the right...that is, not an official right but his own right, to allow his conscience to step over certain obstacles'. His friend Razumikhin lodges a strenuous moral protest: 'you do finally permit bloodshed in all conscience...This permission to shed blood in all conscience is...to my mind more horrible than if bloodshed were officially, legally permitted.' Yet the more searching critique finally issues from Raskolnikov's interrogater Porfiry, who tackles him on his callow claims of exceptionality, and then concludes in the prescient observation that some of these apparently exceptional men might achieve their goal, but then (in words that Raskolnikov supplies for him) 'start doing their own punishing'. Raskolnikov is able temporarily to suppress that regulatory principle in his own mind that would have forbidden his crime, but at a price ('I killed myself, not the old crone'), and his escape from the rigours of conscience is temporary rather than permanent. By way of measuring Raskolnikov's inability to escape from the rigours of his own conscience, Dostoevsky gives us the authentically amoral Svidrigailov, who randomly alternates ethical atrocities and acts of arbitrary generosity, and whose 'conscience is entirely at rest'. This is a stance that Raskolnikov, for all his bluster about 'crossing over' the ethical divide, and for all his Napoleonic fantasies, cannot achieve.

Raskolnikov will, indeed, experience a regeneration in Siberia, at the end of the novel, but his regeneration will not exactly proceed from the 'remorse of conscience' that the faithful (but literal-minded) Dunya imagines for him. Even as he lashes out at himself for his inability to take 'the first step', he still suffers more from wounded pride and chastened critique of his inability to escape his own self-limitations, than from conscience *per se*. His relation to conscience remains ambivalent and conflicted. Even as he seeks to surmount it as a force in his own life, and steadfastly rejects it in the end, it stages a variety of 'returns' throughout the novel. We can read it as a tacit pressure in his early-arriving and never-ending attraction to confession, in the very excesses of his morbid self-critique, and in his final evacuation of his blistered and excessive ego in favour of a humbled and self-abasing love.

Crime and Punishment represents an examination rather than, strictly speaking, a vindication of conscience, and this examination continued in Dostoevsky's writings, especially in his summative *Brothers Karamazov* (1881). One might almost say that the entire novel can be read as an examination of the 'grounds' of conscience. It begins by identifying a traditional 'Karamazov conscience' as shorthand for a superficial and incomplete ethical grasp. It goes on to pose, without ever fully resolving, the question of where and how a more sustainable view of conscience is to be found. Speaking from within the assumptions of organized religion, the Elder offers a traditional but humane view, according to which conscience protects society and holds the potential for individual transformation by virtue of 'Christ's law alone, which manifests itself in the acknowledgement of one's own conscience.' This form of conscience is administered by the Church, and allows an interior reformation which has the potential to 'appease' guilt. This negotiation of responsibility between the institutional Church and the self-critical individual is, however, insufficiently rigorous from the viewpoint of the Grand Inquisitor, apologist for an institution that knows the needs of individual persons better than they can know their own. The Elder's view smacks to him of self-emancipation, and, in its fluidity ('unusual, enigmatic, and indefinite'), to provide no firm foundation for quieting an inherently unsatisfied and unsatisfiable conscience. The Grand Inquisitor proposes a conscience finite, clear in its demands, and reinforced at every point by ecclesiastical authority.

For his own part, the rational (yet precariously stable) Ivan throws his lot more with the Devil than with the Grand Inquisitor. Ivan's colloquies with the Devil are, of course, expressive of doubts and possibilities arising within his own mind. With respect to conscience, this diabolical alternative 'I' may be understood in Freudian terms to offer the most alluring and disturbing alternatives, excused by the sign of negation under which they are expressed. Ivan, in other words, allows himself to say what he actually thinks or fears to be so, under the alibi of its representation as diabolical temptation. With respect to conscience, the Devil picks up where Raskolnikov left off, with the idea that the extraordinary man's task is to free himself from conscience-bound restraints. As Ivan cries to Alyosha,

> He taunted me! And cleverly, you know, very cleverly: 'Conscience! What is conscience? I make it up myself. Why do I suffer then? Out of habit. Out of universal human habit over seven thousand years. So let us get out of the habit, and we shall be gods!' He said that, he said that!

Ivan, however, like Raskolnikov, tempts and torments himself with ideas that he cannot finally support. At his boldest, he claims to the actual murderer Smerdyakov that without God 'Everything . . . is permitted, whatever there is in the world, and from now on nothing should be forbidden.' He cannot sustain such bravado. He is, after all, on the brink of a guilt-ridden and partially self-deceived confession of his own complicity in his father's murder. Other characters praise him for what Alyosha will call his 'deep conscience', and Katya will declare him in the courtroom to be the victim of a self-tormenting 'deep, deep conscience' and will salute him in the end, lying in brain-fever, as a 'hero of honour and conscience'. But these attempts to praise him as an exemplar of conscience seek to impose a residual, traditional view upon a situation that will no longer sustain it. Once the idea of conscience as an invention or construct, an unnecessary and self-imposed burden, has been articulated – even by so compromised a spokesperson as the Devil himself, or even as a discredited alternative within Ivan's fevered thoughts – it will linger as an additional disturbance to an already-challenged concept.

Upon discovery of a French translation of *Notes from the Underground* in 1887, Nietzsche wrote to his friend Overbeck that 'the instinct of kinship (or how should I name it?) spoke up immediately'. Ivan's words to Smerdyakov – 'everything is permitted' – constitute a perfect Nietzschean utterance, and the fact that Nietzsche reproduced these words (even if coincidentally, or *especially* if coincidentally) in his *Genealogy* suggests how much common ground these two thinkers occupied. Nietzsche celebrated Dostoevsky's Underground Man's morbid introspection, and shared his view that the most intense inner pain is self-inflicted – as embodied in the precept of the *Genealogy*, '*you alone are to blame for yourself*'. Upon this precept pivots the whole direction of *ressentiment* as Nietzsche understands it, a diversion of the indictment from recalcitrant external circumstances and inward to an unwarranted but persisting accusation of self. Dostoevsky's self-accusing and self-punishing protagonists present as fine a galaxy of Nietzschean self-accusers as could be imagined.

In Nietzsche's view, conscience abets this act of self-accusation, and thus becomes part of the problem, rather than solution, for mankind. In his *Genealogy*, he argues that, owing to the inroads of religious and social constraints, humankind's natural aggressivity and relish of vengeance was impeded, forced within, and turned against the self in practices of personal torment every bit as cruel as those practised by our most bloodthirsty ancestors. Conscience is the impresario of this introjected self-punishment. 'I regard,' he says, 'the bad conscience as the serious illness that man was bound to contract under the stress of the most fundamental change he ever experienced – that change which occurred when he found himself finally enclosed within the walls of society and of peace.' So confined, and internalizing its frustrations at this confinement, humanity may be seen as an 'animal that rubbed itself raw against the bars of its cage'. Mired in a sense of irredeemable debt and interminable penance, humankind 'invented the bad conscience in order to hurt himself after the more natural vent to his desire had been blocked'.

Of course, Nietzsche's origin-myth is all wrong, and completely unpersuasive with regard to the actual history of the concept. He imagines bad conscience as a modern development, owing to the proscription of the cruelty and festive punishment which previously attended broken promises and contracts, and underwrote the entire justice system. Whereas, in fact, bad conscience – which pricks, gnaws, variously wounds and hectors – was (as I have explained) there from the very beginning, in Roman law and prosecution, and from its earliest Christian adoption. Nietzsche's imagining of an Edenic period when humankind accepted and celebrated its own violence and cruelty and all conscience was good cannot stand either, because conscience first emerged to visibility denouncing bad behaviour and demanding a conversion to something better. As Tillich and others have argued,

an unsettled (and therefore effectively 'bad' state of feeling) is
conscience's default condition, and a 'good' conscience, one that
feels fine about one's deeds, is a sure sign of ethical trouble.

Conscience: troublemaker or second self?

Conscience's identity as an uncanny 'second self' was already well
established when Augustine's conscience verbally assailed him at
the end of the 4th century. Augustine's conscience represented
a split or division, a vantage point from which a person beholds
his or her own actions. In his *Discourse of Conscience* (1596),
theologian William Perkins commented shrewdly on what he
called the two actions of the understanding: 'The minde thinks
a thought, now conscience goes beyond the minde, and knows
what the minde thinks ... By meanes of this second action
conscience may beare witness euen of his thoughts.' His literary
near-contemporary, Shakespeare's Richard III, experiences a
similarly paradoxical division, acknowledging that 'I ... hate
myself / For hateful deeds committed by myself.' In the 18th
century, Adam Smith and Immanuel Kant formalized this
reflexivity, with their theories of an impartial spectator who
knows all about us and who monitors our actions.

At once oneself and another, this second self mingles an
outsider's objectivity and a deep intimacy with our thoughts. This
'second self' provides us with a valued source of ethical
complexity, but at the cost of inner division, of a compromised
sense of oneself as integral and 'whole'. Freud placed this faculty
on a troubling continuum, commenting in 'On Narcissism' that
conscience 'enables us to understand the so-called "delusions
of observation" ... which are such striking symptoms in the
paranoid diseases'. The person of conscience need not be
considered paranoid, and this second self offers a potential source
of equilibrium and balance. But the conscience-stricken individual
knows something of the paranoid's experience of inner division.

Nevertheless, Nietzsche is most certainly onto something, and his insight is similar to what the Devil whispered into Ivan Karamazov's ear: that entry into the regime of conscience is, if not purely voluntary, at least something we do to ourselves. Whether it was there from the beginning, or, as he claims, belatedly self-imposed, bad conscience is something we inflict upon ourselves or, at the very least, allow to be inflicted upon us.

Both Dostoevsky and Nietzsche propose a fundamentally split subject, at odds with a hostile or punitive voice that has already penetrated any defensive perimeter and taken up residence within the mind. Ivan Karamazov hears this voice as belonging to the Devil, although we recognize it as an ungoverned variant of his own; Nietzsche argues that similarly self-harming thoughts are expressed in our own voice, as if they were our own. We are, as he says in the Preface to the *Genealogy*, 'strangers to ourselves' – strangers in the sense that we alienate ourselves from ourselves when we introduce punitive or self-flagellating thoughts as personal or private articulations. He well understands, as Freud will understand, that this punitive voice may introduce itself under the benign guise of correction or chastisement for our own betterment, but that it is simultaneously a source of unending torment.

Nietzsche's comment on conscience is, essentially: get over it! But he doesn't expect us to get over it any time soon. For better or worse (and Nietzsche would certainly say for worse), we are unlikely to succeed in banishing this voice from our heads or ears. How this voice insinuates itself is a subject on which Freud learned a great deal from both Dostoevsky and Nietzsche, and he builds upon their presuppositions in his own theory of conscience as the voice of the punitive father.

Ivan Karamazov is a perfect Freudian subject before Freud. Although he does not actually kill his father, he confesses to complicity in the crime because he has wished his father dead: 'Who doesn't', he says in the course of his trial, 'wish for his father's death ... ?' This, then, is his birth to conscience, his guilty feelings leading him to imagine himself complicit in a crime he did not commit. No wonder that Freud, who considered *Brothers Karamazov* the most magnificent novel ever written, turned to it in his essay on 'Dostoevsky and Parricide'. There, he finds in Dostoevsky an unusually pathological example of one who has taken the prohibitive voice of the father into his own ego, but chafes under its restriction and thus becomes a laureate of parricide. 'It is a matter of indifference,' he says of the novel, 'who actually committed the crime; psychology is only concerned to know who desired it emotionally and who welcomed it when it was done' – in this case, not only the murderous half-brother Smerdyakov, but Dimitri and Ivan as well.

A key Freudian perception is that guilt, and conscience as guilt's abettor, are much freer-floating than we realize, and stand in a different relation to the criminal act than is usually assumed. Rather than a consequence of the criminal act, conscience-induced guilt can be understood in Freud's system as an *incentive* to the criminal act. The subject, experiencing guilt as a consequence of repressed hostility or other dissatisfaction, then commits (or imagines having committed) a crime in order to provide an objective counterpart to the guilty feelings. Which touches upon the subject of Freud's extensive acquaintance with, and admiration for, the writings of Nietzsche, whom he credits (in 'Character-types in Psychoanalytical Work') with the perception that 'guilt precedes crime'. In this indictment, conscience (with its stepchild guilt) is seen less as the resolution or absolution of a transgression, than as fundamental to the transgression itself, as an unappeased dissatisfaction that is more likely to lead to the commission of crimes than to their resolution or satisfaction.

A separate essay would be required to trace Freud's affinities with Nietzsche's ideas about repression and other key concepts, but what I want particularly to consider here is Freud's tacit but very deep reliance upon Nietzsche's theories of self-punitive conscience in the formation of his own ideas about the superego or ego-ideal, with its innate and punitive hostility to the ego and, by derivation, the self. This deep correspondence may be illustrated in a short quotation from each:

> Conscience . . . is not, as you may believe, 'the voice of God in man'; it is the instinct of cruelty, which turns inwards once it is unable to discharge itself outwardly.

> (Nietzsche, 'Why I Write Such Excellent Books', *Ecce Homo*)

> The more a man controls his aggressiveness, the more intense become the aggressive tendencies of the ego-ideal [superego] against his ego.

> (Freud, 'The Ego and the Id')

In each case, a blocked outlet for hostile feelings (cruelty unable to discharge itself, aggressivity under restraint) leads to an inward recoil (cruelty turned within, aggressivity against one's own ego).

Freud's ego-ideal – and, later in his work, superego – operate in the space of conscience for him, and perform the chiding functions normally assigned to conscience. As he puts it in 'The Ego and the Id':

> An explanation of the normal conscious sense of guilt (conscience) presents no difficulties; it is due to tension between the ego and the ego-ideal and is the expression of a condemnation of the ego pronounced by its criticizing function.

The criticizing function is equivalent to the operations of conscience, especially with respect to its operation under the screen of ostensible self-improvement, even as it proves implacable and unappeasable in its demands.

The ego-ideal is, in Freud's view, socially formed, gathering 'from the influences of the environment the demands which the environment makes upon the ego and which the ego cannot always rise to' ('Group Psychology'). In his view, these demands normally, perhaps even invariably, represent an internalization of the views of the parent, but augmented by other constraining and regulatory voices of society as a whole, as described in 'The Ego and the Id':

> As a child grows up, the office of the father is carried on by masters and by others in authority; the power of their injunctions and prohibitions remains vested in the ego-ideal and continues, in the form of conscience, to exercise the censorship of morals.

Arrayed, that is, against the ego is the cumulative force of every kind of prohibition and disapproval the child has experienced in the course of life; in other words, a severe mismatch. As Freud continues, 'The tension between the demands of conscience and the actual demands of the ego is experienced as a sense of guilt.' The ego, in other words, forms itself in processes of social interaction, but is liable to be over-borne by the sheer weight and variety of the limitations and accusations with which it must contend. One may fly to, and take solace from, this part of oneself that watches and judges the ego, but at a cost – at the very least, the cost of self-division.

A possible avenue of reintegration – and here I depart from Freud's own conclusions to reflect upon materials he has placed on view – rests in the fact that, as he says, the faculty of self-observation within conscience or the ego-ideal characteristically speaks in the third person ('On Narcissism'). This is natural enough, since it is a voice compounded of words and perspectives external to the subject, whether drawing upon the voice of parental prohibition or other voices of authority we have heard in our lives. (Mill says in his *Autobiography* that conscience spoke to him in his father's voice, and Mill is hardly alone in this experience.) Wavering between self and other, just as did conscience in the case of Augustine, the voice of authority addresses the subject in the second person ('you must'...) and speaks in the first person ('I must'...) as well. May not a hint of promise reside in this adoption by conscience of a first-person voice? In conscience's adoption of the first person may be seen a possible advance in the maturation of the subject, now ready to narrow or eliminate the gap between the ego and the exorbitant demands of the ego-ideal, and to assume personal responsibility for one's choices and actions.

Such speculations aside, Freud leaves the ego in a parlous plight, seemingly unable to emancipate itself from the dominion of an ego-ideal which 'rages against the ego with the utmost cruelty' ('The Ego and the Id'), generating a sense of inescapable guilt. Freud joins Dostoevsky and Nietzsche in presenting the operations of conscience, in its relations with the self, more as an inescapable dilemma than as a vital human resource.

Conscience survives

In assailing conscience for its tendency to carp and complain, its incessant dissatisfaction with the behaviour it comments upon, its unappeasable stance, these critics of conscience engage in no misrepresentation. These are, after all, traits of conscience observable since its origins in the castigation of Roman criminals. Conscience's critics are simply taking one of its defining tendencies and placing a different valuation upon it, viewing it less as a force for self-remediation and more as needless self-castigation. But even these severe critics find conscience hard to send off. Each, in the end of it all, seems partially to reverse himself, and to grant conscience a certain grudging respect.

Perhaps most surprising of all is a comment of Freud's, that – after all he has said to discredit conscience (and its placeholders, the ego-ideal and the superego) – 'we shall count it, along with the censorship of consciousness and the testing of reality, among the great institutions of the ego' ('Mourning and Melancholia'). But how does this greatness manifest itself, and what is so great about it? To be sure, Freud does suggest that, in some respects, the superego can be a refuge and resort from the truly battered and subjugated ego: 'a man, when he cannot be satisfied with his ego itself, may nevertheless be able to find satisfaction in the ego-ideal which has been differentiated out of the ego' ('Group Psychology'). The super-ego/ego-ideal/conscience can still, that is, under the right set of circumstances, be a force of needed self-regulation and self-esteem. Yet the provision of an occasional 'safe-house' for the stressed ego seems hardly to manifest qualities of greatness – all the more when the hyper-critical super-ego can be considered one of the fundamental enemies of ego-esteem. A more persuasive account of the superego's greatness may be found in Freud's late work *Civilization and Its Discontents* (1930), in which conscience joins sublimation as one of the psychic mechanisms by which an individual binds instinctive (and inherently selfish) desires in a form that – deliberately or not – promotes the general social interest. Not that the restraint of desire by conscience has ceased to be onerous to the individual, but it possesses an incidental – or perhaps even more than incidental – benefit for society. Freud even goes so far as to suggest that the development of a superego, with conscience as its confederate and guilt as the penalty for ignoring its strictures, can be an endeavour of the whole community, and that the community can develop and employ a collective superego to benefit its cultural aims:

> The analogy between the process of civilization and the path of individual development may be extended in an important respect. It can be asserted that the community, too, evolves a super-ego under whose influence cultural development proceeds.

Nietzsche, whose derision towards conscience as a self-imposed and never-ending penance would seem to brook no limit or compromise, also discovers affirmative possibilities for conscience in some surprising corners of his oeuvre. In his anti-Christian screed, *The Antichrist*, he makes the kinds of dismissive comments his reader comes to expect about 'the pangs of conscience' as a part of the imaginary 'sign-language of the religio-moral idiosyncrasy'. But he also allows himself to imagine a purged and perfected conscience, bent not towards craven self-punishment but towards edification, rationality, and enlightened (scientific) values. This sub-discourse enters his essay as an apparently thrown-away wish that Kant had possessed a more thoroughgoing 'intellectual conscience' rather than confusing reason with *a priori* moralization. Yet, as the essay develops, he advances conscience as a vital tool in the unmasking of religious hypocrisies:

> We know, today *our conscience* knows, what these uncanny inventions of the priests and the church are really worth, *what ends they served* in reducing mankind to such a state of self-violation that its sight can arouse nausea.

Arguing for the precedence of science over religion, he longs for the sway of 'the discipline of the spirit, purity and severity in the spirit's matters of conscience, the noble coolness and freedom of the spirit'. In this vision, an emancipated and secularized conscience becomes an arbiter, a rigorous decider of difference, and a tool by which ethical clarity is to be sought:

> What does it mean, after all, to have *integrity* in matters of the spirit? That one is severe against one's heart, that one despises 'beautiful sentiments', that one 'makes of every Yes and No a matter of conscience'.

This idea of redeemed conscience, as a guardian of integrity, must surprise, given all that Nietzsche has elsewhere said. But the strength of conscience has always rested with its surprising motility, its availability to recasting and re-enlistment in new forms and causes. And so, perhaps, Nietzsche's *volte-face* need not surprise us at all.

So too, and perhaps least surprisingly, with Dostoevsky, who toys with the idea that conscience may be invented and unnecessarily self-imposed, but who then arrays his fictions with a variety of characters who are more conscience-driven than they are able to articulate and who display their acquaintance with conscience under a variety of impulses that do not even bear its name. Raskolnikov and Ivan share a common pattern, which is to denounce conscience and toy with schemes to avoid its strictures, even as they reveal themselves as conscience-driven. Raskolnikov, having committed his crime, immediately experiences a desire to confess to the authorities and to display evidence of his crime:

> It was as if a nail were being driven into his skull. A strange thought suddenly came to him: to get up now, go over to Nikodim Fomich [a minor bureaucrat], and tell him all about yesterday, down to the last detail, then go to his apartment with them and show them the things in the corner, in the hole. The urge was so strong he had already risen from his seat to carry it out.

This might seem simply a matter of what Poe called 'the imp of the perverse', a prompting of conscience at its most self-destructive, except that Raskolnikov spends much of the novel in one confessional act or another, and his final desire to 'embrace suffering' seems, at least tacitly if not explicitly, to be conscience-driven. Certainly, others have no hesitation in portraying his predicament as one of conscience, as when Dunya asserts his capacity for 'remorse of conscience' to the end. Similarly, for Ivan Karamazov. For all his personal avoidance of conscience-claims, and ambivalent rejection of conscience, others regard him as a hero of conscience, and he may well be. Certainly, he is something of a hero of personal psychic investigation, his insight that tacit consent in, or implicit wish for, the death of his father is a

74

legitimate cause of guilt is not only Freudian *avant la lettre*, but shows an ethically refined willingness to assume a burden of personal suffering that belies his own dismissive critique.

Thus, implicitly and through a variety of side and back doors, even harsh critics of conscience tend to acknowledge its centrality, and reveal their own unwillingness wholly to set aside the very concept against which they inveigh. This revisionary impulse, in which a thoroughly traduced conscience is suddenly restored to its position of respect, need not altogether surprise us. Earlier, I mentioned the case of Calvin, who said every possible denigratory thing about the insufficiencies of conscience and its inadequacy to the tasks imposed upon it, and then shifted ground to a new vision of Christian Liberty in which conscience is freed from the task of enforcing the Law and purified by the mercy of Christ. Even conscience's severest critics seem not quite to seek its banishment, but ultimately to interest themselves in the imagined conditions of its rehabilitation and return.

Chapter 4
Is conscience a civil right?

Some people seem to get along without any conscience at all, to be endlessly capable of what Locke described as 'enormities practised without remourse'. In the *Tempest*, Shakespeare gives us the villainous and usurping Antonio who is contemplating murder and, asked about his conscience, replies:

> Ay, sir; where lies that? If 'twere a kibe [chilblain],
> 'Twould put me to my slipper; but I feel not
> This deity in my bosom. Twenty consciences,
> That stand 'twixt me and Milan, candied be they,
> And melt ere they molest!

Antonio is found out and mildly punished by expulsion from his usurped duchy, but we are given no evidence of his reform. The idea that everybody has a conscience is surely a generous one, resulting from a wish (that everyone possess a conscience) restated as a conclusion (that everyone possesses one). Certainly, we act on the supposition that most people possess one. The mere suspicion that a malefactor lacks conscience can serve to increase the severity of a sentence, even as evidence (however superficial) of a reformed conscience can inspire leniency.

But once we start supposing that everyone has a conscience, and bases actions and choices upon its advice, another issue arises. If conscience is a good thing, and if people are encouraged to act in response to its promptings, then how much deference is owed to a claim simply *because* it is conscience-based? And, especially, how much deference is owed to a conscience-claim with which we happen to disagree?

Most of us will give some ground to a conscience-claim. One revealing test-case of society's capacity for such toleration is afforded by conscientious objection to military service. Conscientious objection has sometimes, to be sure, been treated as a crime, but equally often, even amidst the passions of wartime, nations have devised forms of exemption or alternative service for those who can demonstrate sustained philosophical or religious objection to taking human life.

Objection to war may be traced in early Christian thought (though it was soon overtaken by theories of 'just war' and rightful crusade), and the cause was revived by 16th-century Anabaptists and Mennonites and 17th-century Quakers. Some early Quakers served in the Commonwealth armies, but the connection between pacifism and the requirements of conscience had certainly been forged when the Quakers organized themselves as the Society of Friends and formalized refusal of military service as one of their crucial tenets. One objecting Quaker, impressed into naval service in the 1660s, left an account of a sympathetic bowswain's mate who came to his defence:

> 'this man,' said he, 'is called a Quaker, and for conscience-sake
> refuseth to act, therefore I . . . do promise before God and man that
> I will never beat, nor cause to be beaten, either Quaker, or any other
> man that doth refuse for conscience-sake to act for the King.'

Quaker influences were also felt in North America, especially in regions like Pennsylvania and Rhode Island where a short-lived but telling resolution in 1673 exempted from military service men 'who are persuaded in their consciences they may not fight to kill'. Conscientious objection was common in the American Revolutionary War, with the movement splitting into two camps that would persist through the following centuries: those who accepted alternative service and those (mostly Quakers) who persevered in unconditional resistance. Conscientious opposition, on the part of Quakers, Mennonites, Brethren, and other non-complying religious groups, was also prominent in the American Civil War. On the Union side, and eventually on the Confederate side, opt-out provisions for conscientious objection were adopted, and, on the Union side, provision was made for alternative service in nursing and hospital care.

Aside from naval impressment, military service was effectively voluntary in England between the Civil Wars until 1916, when debate of the issue became urgent again. Actually, as John Rae has pointed out, the issue of 'conscientious objection' first arose under that name in England, in 1914, not in relation to military service at all, but in describing organized and vehement opposition to mandatory vaccination. The Military Service Bill of 1916 imported the principle of 'conscientious objection', but without strict specification as to which organized body of belief or school of personal thought the objector belonged. Various groups – including Socialists, 'Bloomsburys', and others – were granted some leeway to register conscience-claims unconnected with formal religious observance. The complexity of the criteria by which authentically 'conscientious' objection was to be recognized is illustrated by the mixed performance of Tribunals established to decide upon particular cases. Like the Court of Equity (also called 'Court of Conscience') in the 16th century, these bodies faced the problem of deciding upon what was effectively a matter of inner disposition. Rae cites a Quaker description of the perplexities of testimony before such bodies; testimony in which the applicant was likely to be:

> Passionate and idealistic, sometimes over-stating his case and
> sometimes mis-stating it, sometimes apparently impracticable,
> confused by varying impulses – religious, political, economic, social

– desirous of being loyal to his highest conceptions and continually embroiled in irrelevant discussions about the lowest, and always surrounded by the immense difficulties of a just and reasonable interpretation of his own convictions.

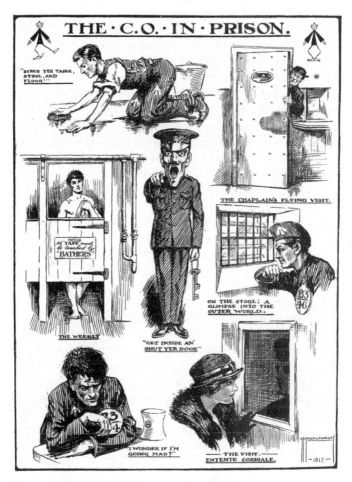

7. 'The C.O. in prison', by G. P. Micklewright, postcard, 1917

The failure of this system is reflected in the inconsistent performances of different Tribunals, and that some 6,000 conscientious objectors either found themselves in military service as the result of receiving no hearing or being refused upon hearing, subsequently to be court-martialled, often repeatedly, and sent to military prisons. Yet, in some respects, this system was an astonishing success, with some 16,500 cases heard and with fully 80% receiving some form of conditional exemption, usually involving alternative service. The system was then further refined in the 1939 Military Training Act, which allowed discharge (rather than imprisonment) for persons who, once inducted into the military, refused service or committed an offence for reasons of conscience. The same general trajectory may be traced in the United States, which during World War I allowed alternative service to those who could demonstrate religious training and pacifist belief (but without a specific restriction to members of historic 'Peace Churches'), then shifted in 1948 to outright deferment for conscientious objectors, then returned to a policy of alternative service during the Korean War.

Even as the general understanding of conscience has expanded to include secular and ethical as well as religious and moral motivations, so have the grounds of conscientious objection shifted to embrace convictions formed outside the boundaries of organized religion. An American Supreme Court decision, for example, opts for intensity of feeling as a measure, in language which has been present in discussions of conscience throughout its history, accepting the principle of exemption for 'all those whose consciences, spurred by deeply held moral, ethical, or religious beliefs, would give them no rest or peace if they allowed themselves to become part of an instrument of war' (398 U.S. 33f). A range of beliefs, some secular, is to be considered in the decision, so long as they 'play the role of a religion in a registrant's life'.

The limits of exemption from military service (or specific duties, in the cases of those already enlisted) nevertheless remain under continuing negotiation. Here arise the cases of those persons who, although not objecting to all wars, experience a particular objection or scruple of conscience with regard to a particular war or a particular category of service. Of course, the more particularized the objection, the greater the likelihood that the matter will fall into dispute. A contemporary instance of 'targeted objection' is the case of Israeli soldiers committed to the defence of their country against common enemies, but confining their service to the 1967 boundaries of Israel and refusing duties in the occupied territories. More recently, counter-claims have arisen on the part of religious conservatives refusing participation in the closure of unauthorized West Bank settlements, or even to serve in the military at all, given the risk that such duties might be imposed. Such matters remain under ardent dispute, in Israel and wherever military conscription is practised. Nevertheless, taken in its entirety, the 500-year history of conscientious objection suggests a considerable willingness on the part of persons in Western societies to accommodate unpopular and hard-to-document beliefs that are understood to possess a basis in personal conscience.

The same may be said about current debates in America over 'conscience clauses', asserting the right of healthcare providers to withhold services – especially abortion-related services, but with more recent extension to all matters of contraception. Various balances between personal conviction and public necessity have been sought, with most of them protecting rights of conscientious refusal by caregivers, while insisting that the interests of patients require swift access to alternative services (without lengthy treks to other hospitals) and safeguards against patient endangerment. Of course, feelings run strongly on both sides, especially between right-to-life Catholics and evangelicals, on the one hand, and seculars and persons of other faiths who insist upon reproductive freedoms, on the other. This matter often comes to a head around particular issues of personal emergency, as in pregnancy prevention and provision of 'morning-after' pills to victims of incest and rape.

The issue of medical caregivers refusing abortion-related services recently flared up in the state of Massachusetts, which has a relatively balanced state statute providing for 'reasonable accommodation' to 'religious needs' of healthcare employees, but insisting that services be provided when the patient's personal health or safety would be compromised by refusal of treatment. This became a 'hot button' campaign issue, with political candidates offering different interpretations of the law. This debate swept into the blogosphere, attracting numerous comments on both sides. A representative pro-choice position was, 'If you cannot in good conscience perform all the duties of a profession, don't enter the profession', complemented by, 'I am tired of my government setting up certain groups of people with rights that do not extend to all equally.' The contrary position was, 'You do have an obligation to say no to immoral laws and orders.' Many intemperate statements were, of course, made, but, even in the superheated medium of anonymous electronic exchange, a striking number of participants sought balance and compromise. 'It seems reasonable to me', said one compromise-seeker, 'to just make sure there is someone at the hospital willing to do the procedure.' 'Dialogue, please', said another. And a third, sounding like David Hume, 'We need a solution we can all agree on and that does the least harm.'

An exchange in the British *Observer* for 5 September 2010 covered similar ground in relation to the views of a sex therapist who refused service to homosexuals on conscience-related grounds. One respondent addressed this matter of 'allowing Christians to opt out of their paid occupational duties for reasons of religious conscience' in these terms:

So when you go shopping in your supermarket the checkouts could be staffed by: a Muslim who won't sell alcohol; a Hindu who won't sell beef; a Jew who won't sell pork; a Catholic who won't sell contraceptives; a Christian who won't sell anything on Sunday; a Wee Free who won't sell sinful music CDs; a vegan who won't sell any animal products; a faith healer who won't sell medicines.

Another respondent exclaimed with frustration, 'Once "conscience" exemptions are permitted, where would they end?' Even given such expressions of exasperation, though, most people – and perhaps even these letter-writers – have shown at least some willingness to accept inconveniences out of respect for conscience-based scruples on the part of service providers, even when they do not subscribe to the views in question.

Seekers after compromise are saying, in effect, that some deference is owed to persons of religious or moral scruple, so long as that deference does not compromise the rights of patients to safe and prompt treatment, or clients to alternative and timely service. In other words, substantial numbers of people are willing to defer, at least to a reasonable and specified degree, to positions with which they do not necessarily agree – or with which they might even strongly disagree – when 'rights' of individual conscience appear to be involved. In this degree of deference, the current esteem for conscience is displayed. All the more tellingly displayed, because, as in conscientious objection to military service, the rights of conscience-based refusal are here extended beyond the simple matter of interior belief, and encompass actual behaviour.

The further question to be confronted is whether decisions about the limits of conscience-based belief, and, especially, behaviour, are to be made on an *ad hoc* or case-by-case basis, within the forum of public opinion, or whether a basis exists for thinking that such protections deserve to be extended as a matter of *right*, enforceable by civil or (as in the EU) collective or even (with respect to the UN) international law.

Conscience and the problem of 'rights'

Issues arising from attempts to elevate freedom of conscience to an enforceable right may be epitomized in the United Nations' *Universal Declaration of Human Rights* (adopted 1948). This *Declaration* includes a strong conscience provision. Explaining that 'disregard and contempt for human rights have resulted in barbarous acts which have outraged the conscience of mankind', it states that *'Everyone has the right to freedom of thought, conscience, and religion.'* This is certainly a laudable document, and in the hands of organizations like Amnesty International and Human Rights Watch has been a crucial force for improvement in the circumstances of victims of political and religious discrimination. Nevertheless, it leaves some questions of interpretation and application unresolved.

One such issue concerns the applicability of an originally Western concept, *conscience*, to a wide range of different cultural circumstances. The intractability of this issue may be illustrated by the problem of language itself, and the interpretative variances which arise when this document is translated into some 375 different world languages. Of course, every human language possesses terms of ethical evaluation and right conduct, but few non-European languages possess exact equivalents to the word 'conscience' as it is used in the contemporary West. One remarkable example, communicated to me by East Asian Language and Culture Professor Lydia Liu, concerns the drafting of the Declaration itself:

> When Mrs. Roosevelt and her committee met to draft the *Universal Declaration of Human Rights* for the United Nations in the 1940s, there were many debates on 'conscience'. An important member of the committee was Dr P. C. Chang, a Chinese playwright and diplomat, who prevailed on the committee to adopt the Confucian notion of *liangxin* [an inherent moral disposition] from

Mencius and, as a result, the English term 'conscience' was actually a translation of Chinese *liangxin* in Article One of the *Declaration*, not the other way around!

Professor Liu adds that Chang's insistence on a merged understanding of *liangxin* and *conscience* was an attempt to forge what she calls a 'master sign', powerfully semiotic and freed from its specifically Christian associations. Evidently, a Western member of the committee argued strenuously against Chiang's proposal, seeking a more explicitly European, and Christian, understanding of conscience. This particular debate, at the

CHAIRMAN   UNITED ST

8. Dr P. C. Chang, China, Vice-Chairman, greets Mrs Eleanor D. Roosevelt, USA, Chair of the Commission on Human Rights. The first session of the Drafting Committee on International Bill of Rights, Lake Success, New York, 9 June 1947

Declaration's founding, suggests the challenges of application created by the 375 languages of the document, in which varied local and traditional interpretations of ethical obligation deviate in culturally specific ways from European norms.

Given the diversity of world cultures, and the languages in which they express themselves, the aspiration to a universally recognized definition and standard of conscience must always fall somewhere short of realization. Its claim for universality rests upon the fallacious and sentimentalized belief in a universal human nature, identical for all times and all societies. In response to such universalist assumptions, and especially those first formulated and promulgated in the West, persons of varied cultures have raised a host of objections. Some, as in the rather modest gulf between *conscience* and *liangxin*, are linguistic, but not simply linguistic since language defines (and is defined by) culture. Others – reaching back to the deep history of conscience – deplore its traditional association with Christian values. Yet others – alert to the more proximate heritage of Enlightenment rationalism – are critical of the tendency for Western ideas of 'rights' in general and conscience-claims in particular to be stated on behalf of the autonomous individual. This concern originates in the fear that an overbalance on individual rights and liberties might lead to an underestimation of the rights of the social totality, and particularly those collective rights founded upon traditional cultural or religious practices. But it arises most sharply when Western nations attempt to export their ideas about individual freedoms and conscience rights to other nations. Legislation on human rights is often, as R. Panikkar has observed, thought by members of non-European societies to be introduced 'in order to find a justification for contravening somebody else's freedom'.

Suppose that an awkward fact is admitted: that any assertion of conscience rights is likely to be based on relative and culturally determined principles, rather than absolute and universal principles, however plausible they may seem. Nor does this problem disappear when the scope of conscience-based activity is narrowed from competing nations and cultures to issues of individual choice within a particular and relatively homogeneous society. I say 'relatively homogenous' because each nation and polity, or even neighbourhood, contains mixed and competing cultural ideas from which differing conceptions of conscience-based behaviour are bound to derive. If nations and cultures have different views of conscientious choice, so will a Western agnostic and a Muslim traditionalist, or a Quaker pacifist and a gun-carrying member of the American National Rifle Association, even when living side by side.

Leaving behind the matter of cultural difference, a further obstacle to the universal acceptance of conscience-claims must be admitted. Sometimes conscience, however well intended, *simply gets it wrong*. Aquinas thought so; *synderesis*, God's gift of rational discernment, does not err, but conscience, which must make hard practical decisions in the world, errs all the time, and even sometimes erroneously abets heresy. In the medieval *Piers Plowman*, Conscience makes the disastrous mistake of admitting the Friars to the castle of Unity, and ends up having to take to the road as a solitary truth-seeker. Modern conscience, encumbered by sentiment and adulterated by bourgeois moralization, stumbles into false reason and ethical compromise. We have already seen Mark Twain's memorable depiction of Huckleberry Finn berating himself for the imagined, but clearly erroneous, strictures of conscience over his assistance to the runaway slave Jim. And, of course, there are always those occasions when conscience is not just compromised, but utterly suborned: misses the mark *entirely*. One might respond that such cases of erroneous conscience aren't conscience at all, but only its chimerical falsification. But the hard fact is that judgements of conscience are not invariably right or invariably good. One need hardly mention the most flagrant example of conscience off the rails: that, as Hannah Arendt explained, the Nazis had no particular problems with their conscience at all, but in fact considered themselves beneficiaries of a 'good' or regenerated conscience – a conscience which, at least in the view of some, underwrote their most damnable transgressions.

Verdicts of conscience, and worldly choices and actions based on conscience, are too often mixed, challenged, and downright wrong to insist that every argument can be settled by playing the 'conscience card'. This is not to devalue its ethical valence, the positive incentive to ethical seriousness that a conscience-claim provides. But the assertion of a 'right' to act upon conscience is better seen as a starting point for negotiation than as its conclusive terminus.

Strengthening a conscience-claim

Depending on the scope and nature of the claim, some assertions of conscience rights are more likely to achieve their objectives than others. Prudent self-limitation is one way of assuring optimal adherence to a conscience-based claim. When the *Declaration* states that 'Everyone has the right to freedom of thought, conscience, and religion', it is referring to matters of inward conviction, rather than to actions taken in the world, and few would now challenge an individual's right to such inner freedom. When John Locke asserted that 'Liberty of Conscience is every man's natural right', he was referring to freedom of thought and inner conviction (rather than action), and his assertion seems irrefutable today.

Yet even this relatively rudimentary battle remains fully to be won. In fact, Locke's own defence of conscience, though restricted to beliefs rather than actions, allowed some serious curtailments. He made no provision whatever for the natural rights of women, for example, and he was emphatic in his denial of the benefits of toleration to 'Mahometans' and Atheists. Although one's 'inner' beliefs might at first appear to be an entirely private matter, coercive states have again and again proven adept at formulating loyalty oaths and required observances designed to expose and pressure such beliefs. The example of Roman state authority, which required early Christians to sacrifice to traditional gods as a way of learning their inner disposition, is a celebrated example of such an encroachment. In *Darkness at Noon*, anti-Stalinist author Arthur Koestler wrote urgently about the Soviet 'show trials' and the success of pre-trial interrogation techniques in creating self-doubt by striking at the foundations of autonomous belief. Coerced confessions and recantations are still common in contemporary societies, and are currently practised in Iran, North Korea, and other states inimical to non-conforming belief. As a result, even the most rudimentary rights of private conviction remain more seriously at issue than might be supposed, and their defence requires constant vigilance.

The real test for the principles of the *Declaration* resides, though, in the next step, when conscience rights are imported into the arena of public (as opposed to purely private) behaviour. Although few would disagree about the absolute right of an individual or a group to conscientious *belief*, conscientious *action* raises more complicated issues. Actions affect others, and depending upon its effects on others, an action may fall short of absolute entitlement to be considered an enforceable right.

No sooner do we extend the notion of conscience-based rights to encompass behaviour, than we must confront the problems arising when one person's conscientious deeds collide with the freedoms and prerogatives of others. This issue has always been present to one degree or another in the discussion of conscience. It found one early and pointed focus in William Tyndale's 1528 *Obedience of a Christian Man*, when he argues on behalf of obedience to lay authority by the Christian who is obliged 'first because of thyn own conscience, . . . [and] secondarily for thy neighbour's conscience', explaining that the two consciences are reciprocal and that actions taken (or omitted) in relation to the dictates of one's own conscience have an inevitable effect upon the consciences of others. Certainly, the rights of any single person cannot be expanded infinitely without colliding with the rights of other persons of contrary disposition, thus creating conflict within the social totality. If concepts of conscience are to be extended from the arena of private belief into the arena of public action, then the task is to discover principles which will command assent by balancing the minimum demands of individual freedom while respecting the responsibility of each society (including societies other than our own) to protect the collective wellbeing of its members.

Henry Shue, a scholar of human rights and international law, usefully defines human rights as 'everyone's minimum reasonable demands upon the rest of humanity'. This subtly poised statement asserts the rights of the individual, but within two major limitations. First, they must be 'reasonable', must stand a test of 'reason', which diminishes the obligation to defer to fanatic or unreasonable claims based on selfish interest or fancied divine afflatus, of the sort Locke described as 'rising from the conceits of a warmed or overwheening brain'. Second, if the process of asserting demands is to involve action in the world (and not just freedom of subjective thought), then these demands must not unfairly curtail the rights of others – must, as Mill would have had it, cause no harm.

On this matter of reasonableness: conscience-claims no doubt fare best when they are connected in some discernible way with matters of common belief. The most severe test of our belief in conscience, like our belief in all matters of civil rights or liberties, comes when we are asked to respect a wildly eccentric claim. Yet the derivation of conscience, as *con* + *scientia*, or knowledge in common, has always suggested that its greatest strength lies in its connection to the shared disposition of a larger community. This was Thomas Hobbes's argument in his 1651 *Leviathan*: that conscience must, in keeping with its etymology, be collective rather than a mere collection of individual, secret thoughts. Seeking a collective basis for conscience, Hobbes settled on the principle that 'the law is the public conscience, by which [the polity] hath

9. Hard-going for conscience: 'Gee, Jiminy Liberal!', cartoon by Martin Rowson, *The Guardian*, 10 May 2010

already undertaken to be guided'. *Contra* Hobbes, contemporary history furnishes us all with instances (in India, in the American South, in South Africa, and in Tiananmen Square) when civil disobedience to a bad law has seemed a virtuous course of action; and in such cases, aroused conscience has been instrumental in pitting itself against bad law. Locke and others have, in this sense, valuably modified Hobbes's position by reminding us that laws repugnant to private conscience can be disobeyed, by people prepared to accept a civil penalty as the cost of principled disobedience – thus laying a valuable cornerstone for practices of civil disobedience. Nevertheless, Hobbes's proposal that law might constitute something like a 'public conscience' is valuable in its suggestion that personal conscience works best when it finds some point of attachment in shared belief.

Its authority bolstered by such indices of public support as law, or institutional religion, or even public opinion or downright 'common sense', conscience will continue to deserve its centrality in our ethical deliberations. This is to say that, so long as it is vitalized by unselfish principle and devoted to the good of all, conscience will deserve its centrality in our lives. But the conditional 'so long as' is the catch here. To say that conscience will thrive *if* supported by reason, law, or good sense is to say everything and nothing at all. However laudably, conscience in this formulation still performs like the stone in stone soup: the stone *plus* carrots and potatoes and onions will brew up deliciously, even as conscience *plus* recognized precepts and clear thought will carry the day. If conscience possesses no inherent content of its own, and depends upon commonsense and collective knowledge for supplementation, or even for its very identity, doesn't it simply vanish as an independent force in the world? What remains invariable and important about conscience *in its own terms*, and what role remains for it to play?

My answer returns to conscience's original role, and, specifically, to the intimate link between conscience and persuasion. This chapter began with instances in which respect for conscience is instrumental in persuading otherwise uncommitted people to grant a degree of licence in 'cases of conscience' involving military service and the medical professions. Yet conscience is also crucially active in another form of persuasion, persuading *oneself* not merely to entertain convictions but to act in matters of conviction.

What is conscience for?

At its best, and most successful, conscience not only drives or activates the attempt to refine belief but also translates belief into action and engagement. Conscience is active on two equally important fronts: in spurring the individual to define his or her beliefs about right conduct and then, crucially, to apply those beliefs to emergent situations. This action-seeking aspect of conscience was acutely described by Thomas Aquinas in his 13th-century *Summa Theologica*.

Thomas distinguishes between *synderesis* and conscience, observing that they are frequently confused. He describes *synderesis* as an innate faculty, a matter of natural habit, which disposes to good and murmurs at evil. It consists in things 'which are naturally known, without any investigation on the part of reason, as from an immovable principle'. Conscience, rather than simply knowing or recognizing, is a matter of *application*, and more particularly the application of knowledge to a particular case. Describing conscience in familiar terms as a motivational force, Thomas goes on to explain that it swings into action in the assessment of personal choices and actions: 'Conscience is said to witness, to bind, or incite, and also to accuse, torment, or rebuke. And all these follow *the application of knowledge to what we do*.' I am less interested at this moment in Thomas's contention that *synderesis* is innate (which I personally doubt), and more interested in his description of conscience as a matter of applying known principles to actual situations. Conscience is, in his view, crucially related to performed actions; might even be described as dormant until called upon to assess contemplated or realized choices or deeds. Thus summoned in concrete situations, when decisions are made or to be made, conscience is assigned a vitally consequential role, at the very centre of ethically informed choice.

Conscience therefore supplies a critical bridge between conviction and action. Suppose you, or I, have a right opinion. You may think you got yours from God; I'm more likely to have gotten mine from 'Doonesbury' or National Public Radio or the *London Review of Books*. But this matter of origin is less important than the question of action, of whether you or I actually translate our opinion into action, and this is the task of conscience: to coax, sway, persuade, threaten if need be, but in any case to see that the right thing is *done*. Good intentions, passively entertained, do not constitute a fully or adequately conscientious response.

The author of a recent book about the discourse of 'rights' considers a range of telling criticisms including its alleged cultural

Aquinas on conscience as 'applied knowledge'

Conscience, according to the very nature of the word, implies the relation of knowledge to something: for conscience may be resolved into *cum alio scientia*, i.e. knowledge applied to an individual case...

The same is manifest from those things which are attributed to conscience. For conscience is said to witness, to bind, or incite, and also to accuse, torment, or rebuke. And all these follow the application of knowledge or science to what we do: which application is made in three ways. One way in so far as we recognize that we have done or not done something; 'Thy conscience knoweth that thou hast often spoken evil of others' (Ecclesiastes 7:23), and according to this, conscience is said to witness. In another way, so far as through the conscience we judge that something should be done or not done; and in this sense, conscience is said to incite or bind. In the third way, so far as by conscience we judge that something is well done or ill done, and in this sense conscience is said to excuse, accuse, or torment. Now it is clear that all these things follow the actual application of knowledge to what we do.

(*Summa*, Part 1, Question 79, Article 13)

relativism, its Western hegemonic bias, and difficulties of adjudication presented by contending rights-based claims. But then (in a slightly embarrassed tone), he confesses to 'a qualified belief that we do need a little human rights just now'. I would say the same about conscience. It's an elusive concept. Conscience enjoys no single set of precepts or body of invariable content all its own. Claims of conscience on the part of those with whom we disagree can be irksome and even noxious. Even so, we all need some of it. I don't know of anyone who wants less of it, for themselves or for others. To be sure, the occasional mad person commits an atrocity in the name of conscience, and such aberrations cannot be avoided. Yet, if we take conscience to be that principle of dissatisfaction which urges action upon a foundation of belief, and which won't allow us to rest until its work is done, then we must grant the necessity for more of it in the world.

Chapter 5
The voice of conscience: is it still to be heard?

It is a very hard Thing to believe, that the worst Men can do
the worst Things without some Sense and inward
Compunction, which is the Voice of their Conscience; but
it is easy to think that they may still and drown that Voice,
and that by a Custom of Sinning they may grow so deaf as
not to hear that weak Voice.

(Edward, Earl of Clarendon, 'Of Conscience', 1670)

Conscience's voice

Conscience originated within the oral traditions of Roman
litigation and pleading, and it retained the character of a spoken
intervention. In Augustine's first, and precedent-setting, encounter
with his conscience, the fact that he heard it as a voice had much to
do with its impact upon him. To return, for a moment, to that
crucial passage:

The day had come when I should be naked to myself and my
conscience mutter within me [*increparet in me conscientia mea*]:
'Where is my tongue?' Indeed you kept saying [*dicebas*] how that
you would not cast off the burden of vanity for an uncertain truth.
Behold, matters are now certain, and you are still burdened...

This passage not only gives us conscience as a voice, but it depicts conscience bestirring itself, literally finding its voice. One of the meanings of Augustine's Latin *increpare* is to 'rustle' and, with respect to speech, to 'mutter' or 'murmur'. This first stirring of conscience is less a fully developed rant than a kind of fumbling towards speech, preliminary to speech itself: a kind of preverbal fuss. Then, with 'Where is my tongue?', conscience lays claim to speech itself. The importance of speech to conscience's realization of itself is figured in a tussle over possession of Augustine's tongue. One translator of this passage renders 'Where is my tongue?' as 'Where is *your* tongue?', and the confusion is understandable. Arriving, as it were, from somewhere outside Augustine's ambit of immediate experience, conscience must secure rights and means of speech if it is to make its influence felt.

Conscience forcibly asserts its right to speak, and will not be denied, but nevertheless speaks as a friend and confidant rather than a usurper or bully. Its words are enunciated within – *in me* – and its effects are felt *intus* or inwardly. Its intimacy is figured in its choice to address Augustine by the familiar Latin *tu* rather than the more formal and peremptory *vos*. For all this intimacy, though, conscience does not forgo the devices of rhetoric and techniques of oral persuasion. It avails itself of such techniques as sarcasm and derisive mimicry, or even both at once, by repeating Augustine's characteristic utterances back to him in mocking tones: its 'You would say' is cast in the Latin tense that suggests a repeated action – 'You are always saying' – and then it reiterates one of Augustine's vain equivocations, about waiting for certainty prior to conversion, in his own tone of voice.

Augustine's conscience's fully formed personality needs a speaking voice to convey its own impatient irascibility, its intimacy, the urgency of its reformative desires. And so has conscience repeatedly availed itself of voice, and vocalization, throughout its long, suasive, and influential career.

In another and later culture, and motivated by a different (and now protestant) religious authority, Daniel Defoe's Robinson Crusoe is addressed by conscience too. Gripped by fever and despair, Crusoe has questioned his treatment by God and receives an emphatic reply:

> My conscience presently checked me . . . and methought it spoke
> to me like a voice: 'Wretch! Dost thou ask what thou hast done?
> Look back upon a dreadful misspent life and ask thyself what thou
> has not done.'

This voice jolts Crusoe into a new frame of mind, and he will eventually restore himself by a self-administered course of tobacco-ingestion and Bible-reading. Cultural differences aside, this conscience still shares many traits of Augustine's. Crusoe's is equally chiding and insistent. It tells him something he already knows, but has been ignoring and must be jolted into knowing. This conscience presses Crusoe forward in a spiritual investigation he had already begun, and in this respect, it seems an extension of his own thoughts, an indwelling faculty. At the same time, it knows things he doesn't, and speaks with an authority that Crusoe alone could never have mustered. In this respect, conscience occupies the same vantage point it did with Augustine, combining an indwelling awareness of situation with an externally derived grasp of what must be done about it.

This ambiguity is evident in Crusoe's response: 'I was struck dumb with these reflections, as one astonished, and had not a word to say, no, *not to answer to myself*, but rose up pensive and sad . . . ' Here we have a situation akin to the wrestling match between Augustine and his conscience for possession of his tongue, a dialogic situation in which 'myself' demands an answer from 'myself'. One party to the dialogue speaks, in effect, for the old or habitual Crusoe; one for the dawning of a new (and at least potentially demanding) awareness. Conscience performs as a second self, like Crusoe but with differing and more secure commitments, speaks in his voice, but a voice altered by responsibilities of mission and command.

In a yet more recent incarnation, Robert Louis Stevenson's story 'Markheim' offers a more ambiguously situated conscience – no longer directly authorized by God and perhaps even capable of slightly diabolical mischief – but a conscience still possessed of traits we will recognize. Stevenson accepts the premise of conscience as a second or alternative self, but carries that idea a step further by granting it not only a voice but, however temporarily, a visage of its own. His protagonist is a murderer who, having consummated his deed, encounters an uncanny figure at once like and unlike himself:

> Markheim stood and gazed at him with all his eyes. Perhaps there was a film upon his sight, but the outlines of the new comer seemed to change and waver like those of the idols in the wavering candle-light of the shop; and at times he thought he knew him; and at times he thought he bore a likeness to himself; and always, like a lump of living terror, there lay in his bosom the conviction that this thing was not of the earth and not of God. And yet the creature had a strange air of the commonplace, as he stood looking on Markheim with a smile.

As with Augustine's and Defoe's conscience, this figure is intimately involved with Markheim, is a kind of second Markheim, but is somehow separate from him as well. Even as Augustine struggles for possession of his own tongue, and Crusoe finds himself drawn into debate with himself, Markheim hallucinates a figure of similarly dialogic impulse, a figure of uncanny 'likeness' who speaks to him in something eerily like his own voice. Stevenson is not the first to create a walking, talking conscience; Conscience is a prominent character in medieval poems like William Langland's *Piers Plowman*, and walks the stage under his own name in 15th- and 16th-century morality plays. And, in all these incarnations, conscience possesses the gift of persuasive speech.

Markheim tries at first to hold his own troubling visitor at bay, a typical response, since conscience is never entirely welcome upon its appearance, bringing not only self-awareness and new knowledge but arduous responsibilities as well.

> 'Be helped by you?' Markheim cries. 'No, never, not by you! You do not know me yet, thank God, you do not know me!' 'I know you', replied the visitor, with a sort of kind severity or rather firmness. 'I know you to the soul.'

Markheim commits the error of entering into dialogue with his similitude, with the result that he is persuaded to confess – a confession that may, or may not, represent his best interest. Upon Markheim's confession, his similitude's job is done; it decomposes, fades away, and we are left wondering about its ultimate intentions on our protagonist's behalf:

> The features of the visitor began to undergo a wonderful and lovely change: they brightened and softened with a tender triumph, and, even as they brightened, faded and dislimned.

Stevenson is less certain or secure than Augustine or Defoe in his estimate of conscience and the divided loyalty or double business to which it is bound; Markheim's conscience's speech is seductive speech, wooing him less to salvation than a form of self-punition. But it does so in words, in persuasive talk.

Although so different in their import, each of these three instances involves a person in an extreme situation, ready for a new resolve, whether conversion in the first two cases or confession in the third. In this sense, we might properly speak of a 'visitation' of conscience, in which conscience assumes the role of a third party possessed of special or 'insider' knowledge of the protagonist's dilemma. Some decades ago, Bruno Snell wrote his brilliant *Discovery of the Mind* in which he shrewdly observed that, when the ancient Greeks needed to explain a major change of outlook or the adoption of a new resolution, they tended to introduce an outside visitation, by a god or anther external agency – an agency familiar with the case at hand, but also possessed of new knowledge or insight or a set of revised demands – and the consequence of this visitation is a mind-changing colloquy, a chance to talk the stalled or troubled person around to a new point of view. Thus a muse, for example, might visit a singer of tales to tell him of new material or a new source of inspiration, or a goddess might persuade young Telemachus to seek his father. We now possess many new languages of psychological process unavailable to the ancient Greeks, including medieval Christian psychomachia or inner struggle, Reformation self-analysis and reflexivity, and Freudian awareness of unacknowledged motive. But earlier descriptions of mind and mental process remain on call as well, and the discourses of conscience enjoy an affinity with the most venerable patterns of psychological explanation, in which a person confronted by an unsolvable dilemma receives a visitation by a privileged interlocutor.

Still lingering is the question of why conscience's visitations are so frequently couched as occasions of direct address. Each of my three examples renders conscience as what might be called a 'liminal' entity, operating simultaneously on the inside and the outside, possessed of an uncanny degree of internal–external knowledge. Conscience thus functions as a participant–observer, mediating between the self and the world. And speech is the appropriate vehicle for such mediation, since mediation between self and other is, of course, the primary task of speech itself. In the act of speaking, we consolidate our selfhood, even as we employ language to display that selfhood to the world. The speech act is itself a common property, bridging the gap between inside and outside, speaker and addressee. As German philosopher Hegel says in his 1807 *Phenomenology of Spirit*:

> Speech is the self-consciousness that subsists for others ... It is the
> self, splitting itself apart, which becomes objective to itself ...,
> maintaining itself as this self just as much as it fuses immediately
> with others and is their self-consciousness.

Hegel's characterization of speech as a 'self-consciousness that
subsists for others' may be applied with equal accuracy to
conscience, and everything we have so far observed of it.
Conscience, like speech itself, connects the private self to the
universal. Speech is, for this reason, its natural medium.

Many of the perplexities surrounding conscience are inherent in its
reliance on speech and language. Language is at once a personal
property and the property of others. Entering into language, we
enter into a medium with a history and a set of inherited
predispositions over which we enjoy less than complete control.
Words, for example, pre-exist the particular uses to which we put
them, and often possess implications unsusceptible to our
purposes. The sense in which language serves our uses, but
temporarily and incompletely since it serves other masters as well,
may be compared with the situation of conscience, which addresses
needs and wishes but with a disturbing detachment. In its own
realization of this communicative channel between inside and
outside, private estimation and public evaluation, conscience may
even be regarded as *a special instance of speech itself*: as internal
speech, serving, as it were, two masters, self and other. In
consequence, it remains a powerful agent of self-realization, but
also an unruly and unpredictable force.

A weakened voice?

Writing in the troubled decades of the 17th century, Edward, Earl
of Clarendon, suggested (in the epigraph to this chapter) that
conscience might continue to speak but in a weakened or muffled
form. The voice of conscience can be drowned in various ways, one
of which is by falling victim to habit (Clarendon's 'custom of

sinning'), or repeatedly yielding to contrary inclination. Worse yet
is the suspicion, evident in Stevenson's treatment of Markheim's
conscience, that conscience might be unreliable or corrupt or its
advice coloured by other interests. Conscience was always sure of
itself, but Markheim's is somehow a little too knowing, too glib, too
evidently in the service of interests other than his own. His is the
sly, seductive voice of the serpent in the garden or Satan in the
temptation of Christ; a voice that invades Markheim's thoughts in
a fashion that leads to his self-destruction.

Mockery and dubious loyalty are traits shared by various avatars of
conscience in the popular media; consciences which tempt, gloat,
and otherwise threaten the destruction of their subjects. I think of
this as a 'Lamont Cranston effect'. A radio programme of my
childhood featured Cranston as 'the Shadow', a latterday
conscience-figure, and its tagline was, 'Who knows what evil lurks
in the hearts of men? The Shadow knows!' Followed by a mocking
'heh-heh-heh'. Certainly, the Shadow had the high ground, since
the victims of his mockery were (like Markheim) undoubted evil-
doers. But something in the Shadow's malicious mirth disallowed
any idea that his goal was to foster moral perfection. The Shadow,
in turn, has a number of epigones in the genre of teen horror films,
in which an unseen or disguised figure mocks his victims with
suggestions of 'I know what you did', or, more specifically, 'I know
what you did last summer'. A voice, speaking from a vantage point
outside the self, but with uncanny knowledge of the self, possesses
a special knack for creating personal havoc and distress. Knowing
all about us, it remains unapologetically aloof from our self-
interested schemes. Thus, one of conscience's persistent traits –
that it is unlikeable, cannot be bribed or bought, and remains aloof
from the persons in which it interests itself – might explain
something of its partial undoing.

Conscience continues to do what it has always done, and at varied
cultural levels, but it has come to enjoy diminished respect. Its call
is still to be heard, but its speech seems often to be muffled,

obscure, or emptied of persuasive or admirable ethical content. In certain philosophical quarters, it still possesses a voice and a call, but cannot escape the suspicion that its call is an empty one – a call of self to self, to self-awareness – as has always in some sense been true – but now a call somehow enclosed within the self, heard by the self alone, devoid of the kinds of manifest content that could guarantee its robustness and its social importance. In the system of 20th-century philosopher Martin Heidegger, the call of conscience is inherently empty, more concerned with self-differentiation of the self from the multitude than with any characteristic ethical content: 'Conscience calls the self forth from its lostness in the they.' The call of conscience hails the self to ethical awareness, yet (perhaps appropriately to the problematic of Heidegger's own soiled career) remains unspecified with respect to the content of that awareness.

Today's self-obsessed – one might say Heideggerian – man of conscience is well represented by Clamance in Camus's *The Fall* (*La Chute*, 1956), a character whom Camus elsewhere described as 'the exact illustration of a guilty conscience'. Clamance's conscience is constituted by a 'cry' uttered by a woman drowning herself in the Seine, a cry which 'waited for me until the day I encountered it' and to which 'I had to submit and admit my guilt'. This is a cry to which Clamance was initially unable to respond, and his inability to respond to it – even to know whence it has issued or what it wants from him – now debars his return to an untroubled life. His predicament is hardly an advertisement for the redemptive powers of conscience; we encounter him, and leave him, in a state of paralysis and debilitation.

The voice of conscience, however, still struggles against odds to make itself heard. As in, for instance, Eminem's hip-hop milestone 'Guilty Conscience', in which conscience is heard, and even rather prestigiously presented, but enjoys only limited success. Eminem, North American rapper and exponent of latterday oral culture, has composed a multi-voiced performance suite in which several conscience-less social actors are egged on by Eminem (as spokesperson of street culture and baser instinct) and restrained by hip-hop mogul and elder statesperson Dr Dre (in the role of conscience).

In the first of three scenarios, we are introduced to Eddie, on the brink of robbing a liquor store:

[Announcer]
Meet Eddie, twenty-three years old,
Fed up with life and the way things are going,
he decides to rob a liquor store.
[Eddie]
I can't take this no more, I can't take it no more homes.
[Announcer]
But on his way in, he has a sudden change of heart,
And suddenly, his conscience comes into play...
[Eddie]
Shit is mine, I gotta do this... gotta do this.
[Dr Dre]
Alright, stop.
[Eddie]
Huh?
[Dr Dre]
Now before you walk in the door of this liquor store
and try to get the money out of the drawer
You'd better think of the consequence.
[Eddie]
But who are you?
[Dr Dre]
I'm your motherfuckin conscience...

Eminem (as Slim Shady), steps in to counter conscience's good advice, proposing in this case that Eddie steal the money and 'Shoot that bitch'.

Dr Dre, as voice of conscience, is very much of our moment: persuasive on the one hand, but a bit wheedling and not all that hard to brush aside. Arguing with Slim over Eddie's soul, conscience finally makes an old-school argument about prudence and consequences ('Yeah but if it all goes through like it's supposed to/ The whole neighborhood knows and they'll expose you'), of a sort unlikely to carry the day in the less receptive world of gangsta rap. Offering up cautionary homilies to Eminem's problematic protagonists, Dre as conscience doesn't do all that well. Stripped of divine warrant, conscience is himself vulnerable to *ad hominem* attack, as when Slim 'names' him and cites his mixed autobiography:

> Mr Dre? Mr N.W.A?
> Mr AK comin' straight outta Compton....
> How the fuck you gonna tell this man not to be violent?

Paradoxically, this mention of Dre/conscience's violent past almost restores his credibility, but finally everything about conscience seems a bit threadbare, up to and including the fact that this role goes to Dre, a venerable figure but now something of a rap *éminence grise*. We still recognize his/her voice when we hear it, and applaud its measured argumentation, but it doesn't have the old punch that commanded pallor, trembly knees, and all the other symptoms besetting conscience's victims in days gone by.

Voice's competitors

A fading voice of conscience can always be amplified, as it is for Shakespeare's Richard III. On the brink of Bosworth, and tormented with bad dreams, Richard hears his conscience speak with a thousand tongues: 'My conscience hath a thousand several tongues,/ And every tongue brings in a several tale,/ And every tale condemns me for a villain.' Even multiplied or at heightened volume, voice alone does not always do the job; Richard, brushing conscience aside as 'but a word that cowards use', is a case in point.

He is lost to conscience, but, in other cases when the voice of conscience is muffled or stilled, other communicative resources may be called into action. Writing and visual imagery have often furthered conscience's aims, although their relation may at times be competitive as well as collaborative.

One of conscience's unruly, but valuable, allies is the written word. Conscience has always had a certain affinity with writing. As early as the Book of Daniel, where the fingers of a man's hand write upon Belschazzar's wall, the idea that an ethical demand might assume written form was abroad. To be sure, the mysterious hand in Daniel inscribes a prophecy, bearing on the overthrow of the king, rather than a personal injunction. But the king's somatic response – in which his countenance is transformed, and his thoughts troubled, and his knees knock together – displays all the signs which traditionally accompany an onslaught of conscience in subsequent Christian tradition. Although Hebrew didn't yet have a single word for conscience, the implicit connection of this magical writing with the dictates of *conscientia* would eventually be made and re-made. In a popular 17th-century treatise entitled *The Book of Conscience Opened and Read*, John Jackson links the handwriting of Daniel (the 'dictates of conscience upon a wall, the wall of Conscience'), together with the wall of brass which resists needless self-condemnation, and the Book of Conscience itself. Throughout its tradition, conscience has sought to get itself, and its principles, engraved or written down.

So vigorous was the idea of a 'book' of conscience that it divided itself into multiple traditions. According to one tradition, the book of conscience is God's own book, to be opened at the time of judgement, a ledger or book of testimony, in which one's deeds are written, as in Revelations 20:12, in which the book of life is consulted in order to perform judgement upon souls standing before the throne of God:

> And I saw the dead, great and small, standing in the presence of
> the throne, and the books were opened, and another book was
> opened, which is the book of life, and the dead were judged by those
> things which were written in the books according to their works.

In the iconography of the Eastern Church, in the tradition of
Deësis mosaics culminating in the splendid example in the Hagia
Sophia, this is the book which Christ holds in his hand. This is the
authoritative book of Jeremiah Dyke's 17th-century *Good
Conscience*, in which he declares:

> Conscience is a booke, one of thse bookes that shall bee opened at
> the last day, and to which men shall bee put, and by which they
> shall be iudged.

An alternate tradition, abetted by new emphasis upon confessional
interiority after the 13th century and by emergent secular practices
of written record-keeping, envisages many books, one for each
Christian, in which his or her conscience acts as scribe throughout
the time of life, maintaining a faithful transcript of deeds. This
view is well established in Dan Michel's early 14th-century
Ayenbite of Inwyt, in which the errant Christian can find his or her
sins enumerated in 'the boc of his inwyt: banne ine ane ssepes
scinne' ('the book of conscience, bound in parchment or a sheep's
skin'). This is also the 'book of reckoning' which Death will demand
from Everyman in the 15th-century morality play. Look, says
Dethe, that

> ...thy boke of counte [account] with thee thou bringe...
> And loke thou be sure of thy rekeninge [reckoning],
> For before God thou shalte answere and shewe
> Thy many bade dedes, and good but a fewe.

Everyman declares his book unready to be shown and asks twelve
years to set it right – years he is not, obviously, to be given. This
tradition, in which each individual Christian conscience compiles

10. The resurrected dead face judgement, each displaying a
personal 'book of conscience', 15th-century fresco, Albi Cathedral

his or her book as a matter of permanent record, is illustrated in the Doomsday depictions of the late 15th-century mural in the Cathedral of Albi, in which we see the damned roiling around with their incriminating volumes and a procession of the saved proudly presenting theirs before the throne: 'In conspectus throni libri aperti sunt' – 'In the sight of the throne, the books are opened'.

The common denominator of these traditions is that the individual conscience, collecting observations in a single and highly personalized volume, will finally turn that volume, and its evidence, to general account. In his 14th-century *Piers Plowman*, William Langland gives us a Conscience who serves, in one of his capacities, as 'Goddes clerk and his notarie', operating from a bastion within the self but transcribing notes on individual conduct for presentation at God's final tribunal. These individual books will all constitute so many instalments of a final, collective anthology, which Robert Burton, in his *Anatomy*, describes as 'a great ledgier booke, wherein are written all our offences, a register to lay them up'; other accusers daunt our morale, but 'it is conscience alone which is a thousand witnesses to accuse us'.

Thus, scriptorial conscience is an inherently divided operator, a kind of double agent, a trusted counsellor simultaneously on somebody else's payroll, an interlocutor who returns to his quarters and writes down what he knows about us and displays it, in written form, to a Final Judge. Like voice, which sits at the boundary of inside and outside, written conscience can work for or against its subject. This doubleness is on display in Andrew Jones's 17th-century *Black Book of Conscience*, in which conscience serves as God's 'Vice-gerent in the soul', taking written notes for future purpose: 'There is a Conscience in every man, that sees and observes, and takes notice of all his ways, and will keep a just account of them, and so be a witness, either for or against the soul at the day of judgment.' Its witness will, again, be presented in the form of a book: 'Conscience takes notice of all thy wayes ... and setteth all down in this *Black Book*.'

In keeping with the tendency of written record to elude or even escape the control of the transcriber, conscience (which advises for one purpose and records for another) runs a partially covert operation, out of a repertoire that includes downright spy-tricks. In Edward Reynolds's 17th-century *Treatise of the Passions*, conscience 'hath...an Eye to looke in secret on whatsoever wee doe', and records its findings in invisible ink: 'That writing in it which seems Invisible and Illegible, like letters written with the juice of Lemmon, when it is brought to the fire of Gods Iudgement, will be most cleere.' Despite the mixed loyalty of its producers, and the ever-present possibility of divergent interpretation, writing stands forth in the end, incradicable and absolute: conscience's censures 'are written with Indelible Characters, never to be blotted out'.

The idea of writing as a solidification of conscience endures. The definitive modern proponent of written conscience, or achievement of conscience through writing, is, of course, James Joyce, whose *Portrait of the Artist as a Young Man* (1914–16) demonstrates, throughout, the process by which writing abets the formation of true conscience. So decided is Joyce's preference for the written word that, for him, conscience achieved in writing competes with, and finally takes precedence over, conscience as expressed in speech. For Joyce's Stephen Daedelus, writing must prevail over the cacophony of voices by which Stephen is constantly assailed:

> ...he had heard about him the constant voices of his father and his masters, urging him to be a good catholic above all things.... He had heard another voice urging him to be strong and manly and healthy...and yet another voice had bidden him to be true to his country.... A worldly voice would bid him to raise up his father's fallen state by his labours, and, meanwhile, the voice of his school comrades urged him to be a decent fellow.... And it was the din of all these hollowsounding voices that made him halt irresolutely.

Foremost among these voices is that of traditional conscience, an institutional position articulated by a sermon delivered within the novel: 'You had time and opportunity to repent and would not...'. These paralysing voices may be likened to Freud's superego, an internalized voice, effectively parental in origin, alien to the subject in its implacable demands ... and hence, for Joyce, a voice or voices to be superseded. Pivotal for Stephen is yet one more voice, one that speaks directly to his soul, 'the call of life to his soul not the dull gross voice of the world of duties and despair, not the inhuman voice that had called him to the pale service of the altar'. This voice enjoins and authorizes the creative artifice of the written word. For writing is the medium in which he will address the more traditionally formed consciences of his Irish peers: 'How could he hit their conscience or how cast his shadow over the imaginations of their daughters ... ?' The renowned answer is, of course, 'I go to encounter for the millionth time the reality of experience and to forge in the smithy of my soul the uncreated conscience of my race.' Conscience here possesses a dual sense derived from the deep history of the word: both 'consciousness' and 'conscience' – the two senses merged in the single word 'conscience' prior to the 17th century. (What Joyce, of course, knows is that every word continues in some sense to mean everything it has ever meant.) Along with 'consciousness', Joyce means 'conscience' too, and for Joyce its privileged medium is writing rather than speech.

Vocal and written conscience may also be augmented – and sometimes rivalled – by more documentary and visual incentives to conscience-based response. In this form, rather than in the spoken or written word, conscience is embodied in depiction: depiction as painting, or engraving, or as photograph bound in a book, but also, and especially, in newer and more instantaneously urgent forms of electronic reproduction.

Visual incentives to conscience have a long history. Later medieval images of the Crucifixion, together with comparable traditions in Baroque and South American art, unsparingly detail Christ's sufferings in order to solicit a human and penitent response. These images often sharpened their demands on the viewer by mixing media, adding poems and inscriptions informing the viewer that these pains were endured for his or her sake, and demanding personal reformation. The chancel arches of many medieval churches were painted with crucifixion scenes in which the eyes of the crucified Christ appeared, uncannily, to focus directly upon each parishioner, inciting a personal response to the suffering depicted there. Goya, Barlach, Kollowitz, Dix, and a host of other visual artists have sought to stir conscience and incite pacifistic sentiment by their unstinting representations of wartime atrocities.

The viewing of a carved crucifix or wall painting or etching shares some common ground with the reception of a photograph or other cinematic or digital image, but mechanical and electronic reproduction also raise new issues of intensity, rapidity, and sheer *scale*. New forms of availability, quantity, and ease of reproduction have greatly enhanced the status of the visual image as a product of, and incentive to, conscience. A mobile phone photograph is flashed around the world in minutes and seconds, unpredictable but potentially vast in its effects.

Such rapidity and multiplicity of reproduction, and swiftness of impact, are quite compatible with a view of conscience that has always been implicitly present, but has achieved additional authority in the last few hundred years: that it expresses itself not in quiet consideration but in a flash of sudden and intuitive insight. As over against a theorist like Joseph Butler, who, in the 18th century, regarded conscience a product of sustained reflection in a 'cool hour', others have regarded conscience as an innate or intuitive faculty, sudden in its apprehensions and peremptory in its demands. The subject of Holman Hunt's *Awakening Conscience* has, for example, obviously experienced such an onslaught. Modern media, in which images surge up and disappear, are, of course, quite congenial to this view of conscience as a more hasty (though no less certain) conviction.

A photograph or image, even an electronic one flashed from cell to screen, shares with voice and word the power to summon conscientious response. In some cases, an image's summons may be the product of an intention – the intention of a speaker or an author or a documentary photographer. Robert Coles, for example, describes the documentary impulse as founded in the conscience of the documentarian. He gives us a James Agee 'excited and challenged by the commands and demands of both his aesthetic sensibility and his conscience'. He describes the camera as a 'weapon', an 'instrument', and a 'call to service' – all wielded by a purposeful and conscience-driven photographer. Yet the photograph, once taken and circulated, also has a remarkable capacity to divorce itself from intention – or, even if it manifests an original intention, to do its work independently of that impulse. Contemporary theorist M. J. T. Mitchell imagines artworks that *themselves* desire things, have designs upon their viewer, work their own kinds of 'Medusa effects'. As Mitchell recognizes, the photographer, of whatever intention, leaves the photograph to do its job. Of course, this is also true of a speech once spoken and a book once written, but an image, flashed instantaneously around the world, is even less closely associated with its maker's intention. Whatever the intention of its maker, it will finally be taken up, or not, as a result of the audience's response. The voice of conscience thus receives important augmentation from print and newer media ... but may also run a risk of alteration, or even dilution, in the process.

Conscience dims: Abu Ghraib

A contemporary muffling of conscience, in forms that come perilously close to outright silencing, is apparent in reports of the Abu Ghraib atrocities. Voice, print, and image are all brought into play, but invariably with skewed effect.

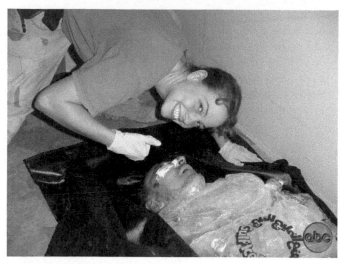

11. Sabrina Harman, doing a 'thumbs-up' gesture beside the body of detainee Manadel a-Jamadi in Abu Ghraib prison

Consider the case of Sabrina Harman, the woman who took most of the Abu Ghraib photographs. She also occurs as a subject in several of them, doing her signature 'thumbs-up' signs next to abused corpses. On view, she would appear to come close to a status fleetingly considered at several points in this book, that of a subject without conscience. Yet Harman reveals herself as a modern subject of conscience, still troubled by various of its simulacra, and as uneasy in her conscience-less state.

Her photographs did not, of course, originate in any kind of conscience-based initiative at all. Their impulse is documentary, not in the tradition of Coles or Agee, to be sure, but in the way that uploaded Facebook party photos seek to document transgressive hilarity and outrage, or that high school students now circulate mobile phone pictures of salacious overindulgence. That being said, there's something about the objectification of a photographic image that can provoke explanation or even encourage reconsideration. Consider Harman's own account of the origins of her documentary impulse:

> I can't get it out of my head. I walk down stairs after blowing the whistle and beating on the cells with an asp to find the 'taxicab driver' handcuffed backwards to his window naked with his under-wear over his head and face. He looked like Jesus Christ. At first I had to laugh so I went and grabbed the camera and took a picture. One of the guys took my asp and started 'poking' at his dick. Again I thought, okay that's funny then it hit me, that's a form of molestation. You can't do that. I took more pictures now to 'record' what was going on.

Something along the lines of self-correction seems to be happening here. Her initial responses of mirth are redone and become transmuted into other sorts of action. She defers or deflects responsibility by grabbing her camera and taking pictures. Actually, her first photograph is one of those gestures of 'predatory' triumphalism that Sontag describes in her 1977 *On Photography* ('At first I had to laugh so I went and grabbed the camera and took a picture'). But her considered impulse is to take pictures 'to "record" what was going on'. This falls somewhere short of a plan to stir conscience in others. 'I just', she says another time, 'wanted to document everything I saw'. And, again, 'If I come up to you and I'm like, "Hey this is going on", you probably wouldn't believe me. . . . So if I say, "Hey this is going on. Look, I have proof", you can't deny it. I guess.' The thing about this kind of documentation is that it goes only halfway towards a conscientious response: that it permits, but requires, no further action. Her impulse was 'Just show what was going on, what was allowed to be done.'

In her phrase about 'what was allowed to be done', we have a hint of the larger situation of ethical crisis in which these events played out: the dereliction of senior officials, the absence of a restraining community – or, worse still, the presence of a complicit one. Still, alongside or underneath the obvious levels of Harman's strategic remorse and evasive blame-shifting, a belated and after-the-fact groping towards some kind of ethical stance might be discerned here. The situation offers us a crowded motivational scene, in which the impulse towards visual documentation jostles with triumphalism, misplaced mirth, Facebook exhibitionism, tourism, sensationalism, sexual titillation, sadism, and a host of other prompts and provocations. It's hard, in other words, to disentangle the impulse to document conscience from a host of other incentives to 'visual' representation. Nevertheless, even when originating as recreation, picture-taking seems somehow, at least slightly, to have composed the ethical mind.

A similar progression may be seen in the case of whistle-blower Joe Darby. Darby also goes through a process that began in misplaced mirth, and cycled through an experience of unfamiliar unease, and culminated in an ethical moment ('it just didn't sit right with me') and a decision to turn the pictures in to such authorities as could be found in that infernal location:

> I was flipping through them, checking out pictures he had taken in Hilla, where we were stationed before Abu Ghraib, when all of a sudden these other pictures came up. And to be honest, at first I thought they were pretty funny. I'm sorry, people can get mad at me if they want, but I'm not a Boy Scout. To me, that pyramid of naked Iraqis, when you first see it, is hilarious. When it came up out of nowhere like that, I just laughed. I was like, 'What the fuck?! I'm looking at a pyramid of asses!' But some of the other pictures didn't sit right with me. The ones of prisoners being beaten, or the one with a naked Iraqi sitting on his knees in front of another naked Iraqi, some of the more sexually explicit-type stuff to humiliate the prisoners – it just didn't sit right with me. I couldn't stop thinking about it. After about three days, I made a decision to turn the pictures in.

His description of the pictures 'not sitting right' and eliciting his corrective intervention might originate somewhere outside the 'conscience' tradition, in the adherence of the American hero to his 'code', his sense of fittingness. Characters like Cooper's Natty Bumppo, and Huckleberry Finn, and countless solitary Westerners like Shane and William Munny in *The Unforgiven*, fall back, in the end, on their sense of a book of unwritten rules and compacts not to be broken, and Darby's relatively laconic explanation for his act might be viewed in this light. Still, it has the marks of conscience upon it, and specifically conscience as stirred by an image bearing irrefutable proof that unacceptable behaviour has occurred. Darby himself doesn't apply the word 'conscience' to his experience, but interviewer/author Wil S. Hylton does, assigning the title 'Prisoner of Conscience' to his article.

Something in the pictures that 'didn't sit right', acted as an irritant, a prick, a goad to an action that Darby had not initially contemplated but finally took. Just as something in the act of recording, objectifying, the events permitted Harman to view the prisoners' treatment as a form of 'molestation'. But where, then, is the perspective, or voice, of conscience in all this? I said that it would be muted, and it is. But it might be barely audible in her comment about 'molestation' – a judgemental term that seems not originally her own, that might have lingered from an early and incomplete training session, or been supplied by a defence lawyer. And it is also dimly to be heard in Harman's iterated 'You can't do that', a voice issuing from without but heard within, a voice of belated prohibition. To be sure, this voice's belated entry smacks of a certain ethical convenience, reminiscent of those Nixon Oval Office tapes in which, discussing matters associated with Watergate, he proposes malicious schemes and then, remembering that he is on tape, hastily adds, 'But that would be wrong'. Nevertheless, a voice of belated prohibition might be better than no voice at all.

If heard at all, the voice of conscience at Abu Ghraib was but weakly and belatedly heard, leading to an attenuated result. The whole point about full-voiced *con-scientia* was that, as its etymology would suggest, it involved a knowing-in-common, a community of social or ecclesiastical opinion that coaxed and chided the potentially errant individual to modify his or her conduct. This was true for the Romans, for the medieval church, and, in revised and restated form, for Adam Smith and for the utilitarians. Yet the voice Harman hears is a lonely and isolated voice, and speaks for no identifiable collectivity at all.

The Abu Ghraib underlings were left to operate in a disturbing sociocultural vacuum, akin to that described by novelist William Golding in *Lord of the Flies*, in which English schoolboys deteriorate in the absence of social supervision. The documentary impulse was a compromised one, and, at best, an end in itself rather than a prelude to action, and the recourse to print media (via journalistic interviews) was more for purposes of self-exoneration than conscientious testimony. Most seriously, the voice of 'You can't do that', stands in the *place* of conscience, but is no longer called 'conscience' and lacks the authority granted to conscience in its varied traditions. It doesn't suffice as a prohibition, and it no longer constitutes a 'call' in any sense we have come to expect. Conscience's 'call' is, at least ideally, addressed to a possible agent, somebody who might actually DO something, whereas the activities at Abu Ghraib occur in agency's black hole.

Abu Ghraib is, of course, a limit case, as unpropitious a place as can be imagined to listen for the voice of conscience, or search for conscientious documentation or written incentives to conscience. I've come back from this brief investigation with some gleanings, but small gleanings indeed. More heartening instances can be found, in which the voice of conscience resounds more emphatically in moments of ethical crisis and painful decision. Lasantha Wickramatunge, a courageous Sri Lankan journalist, recently gave his life to expose corruption. He wrote a farewell report, which amounted to his own obituary letter, which concluded, 'There is a calling that is yet above high office, fame, lucre and security. It is the call of conscience.' Explaining his vote in favour of a faltering gay marriage bill, Fred W. Thiele Jr, a Republican member of the New York State Assembly, explained, 'There's that little voice inside of you that tells you when you've done something right, and when you've done something wrong... That little voice kept gnawing away at me.' Salman Taseer, governor of the Punjab province in Pakistan, declared in a 1 January 2011 television interview that 'If I do not stand by my conscience, then who will?' – three days before his assassination. Anh Cao, the sole Republican Congressman to vote in support of the embattled American healthcare bill, and marked for defeat in the next election, explained, 'I had to make a decision of conscience based on the needs of the people of my district.' Others, daily, make hard choices on conscience's behalf. But the voice of conscience is often, as at Abu Ghraib, only dimly and diffusely heard, its transformative energies muffled, scattered, misspent.

Perhaps conscience is always in crisis; the occasion of crisis is, after all, the medium in which it lives, in which it is summoned and arrives or fails to arrive. But conscience today, severed from its traditional roots in Roman virtue and Christian morality and Enlightenment philosophy, and adrift in a world rich in occasions of abuse, may be more threatened than it ever was. I have already conceded that conscience has what might be called an 'identity problem' – that it possesses no fixed or inherent content of its own, and that it can be hailed and mobilized in defence of one position or equally in defence of its rival. Other societies have functioned ethically without conscience at all. So what would be lost, really, if we were to find ourselves conscience-less, like Shakespeare's Antonio who did not feel any such deity in his bosom, and who considered it of less importance than a chilblain on his toe?

An ethical person does not necessarily need the vocabulary or traditions of conscience in order to be shocked and offended by the sight of a naked, shackled, hooded, abused human figure isolated from human support and subject to every kind of indignation and ridicule; every ethically estimable member of *any* society would obviously decry such a spectacle, in the words and concepts that his or her culture made available. In fact, Western traditions of conscience cannot be said to have served the protagonists of Abu Ghraib well, either in the case of those corruptible enlisted personnel who performed so basely, or of an officer class or government permissive towards, or even encouraging of, such actions. But conscience remains the ethical field upon which, for those in Anglo-American and European traditions, a cry of indignation is most likely to be raised. When traditions of conscience grow weak and, as at Abu Ghraib, its voice is unheard or dimly heard, we will all be ethically the poorer.

I suggested at the end of the previous chapter that the particular strength of conscience is its commitment to remedial action. If measured by this standard, Abu Ghraib must of course be judged a ghastly failure. No ranking officers were disciplined; the prison was closed only to be reopened under other auspices; new forms of coercive detention have been endorsed by the current American administration; nobody knows what happened to the abused 'taxi driver'. If conscience is to thrive and to be worthy of its own best and strongest traditions, then it must consist not only in strong intuitions of aversion, but must re-learn or learn anew the capacity to express itself through actions as well.

Publisher's acknowledgements

References

Introduction

Henry Chadwick, *Some Reflections on Conscience: Greek, Jewish and Christian* (London: Council of Christians and Jews, 1968). I am indebted to conversations with Robert Alter of University of California, Berkeley, on the Hebrew conscience and the etymology of *matzpun.*

Philip J. Ivanhoe, *Ethics in the Confucian Tradition* (Indianapolis: Hackett, 2002); *Confucian Moral Self-Cultivation* (Indianapolis: Hackett, 2000). I am indebted to conversations about *liangxin* with Lydia Liu of Columbia University, and also Xiao Han.

On *al-zājir*, see D. S. Margoliouth, 'Conscience (Muslim)', in *Encyclopaedia of Religion and Ethics* (New York, 1908).

I am indebted to Cathy Popkin of Columbia University for her observations on Russian *sovest.*

Chapter 1

My comments on *syneidesis* are informed by Dominic Mangiello, 'Conscience', in *A Dictionary of Biblical Tradition*, ed. David L. Jeffery (Grand Rapids, MI: Eerdmans, 1992). Also see Mangiello's excellent summary of traditions of conscience in works of English literature.

Peter of Celle, 'On Conscience', *Selected Works*, tr. Hugh Feiss (Kalamazoo, MI: Cistercian Publications, 1987).

A. V. C. Schmidt (ed.), *Vision of Piers Plowman: A Critical Edition of the B-Text*, 2nd edn. (London: Everyman, 1995).

Derek Pearsall (ed.), *Piers Plowman: A New Annotated Edition of the C-text* (Exeter: University of Exeter Press, 2008).

John Wyclif, Sermon 49, in *Sermones, Latin Works*, vol. 7:3 (London, 1890).

On Fisher's rejoinder, see Richard Rex, *The Theology of John Fisher* (Cambridge: Cambridge University Press, 1991).

More's letters are cited from *The Correspondence of Sir Thomas More*, ed. Elizabeth Frances Rogers (Princeton: Princeton University Press, 1947). Henry's *Censurae* are printed in *The Divorce Tracts of Henry VIII*, ed. Edward Surtz and Virginia Murphy (Angers: Moreana, 1988). Other period documents are cited from *Letters and Papers ... of the Reign of Henry VIII*, vols 4:1 and 5 (The Stationery Office, 1878–80).

Luther's words are quoted from *D. Martin Luthers Werke, kritische Gesamtausgabe*, vol. 7 (Weimar: Böhlaus, 1897).

On Luther and Erasmus, see *Luther and Erasmus: Free Will and Salvation*, ed. E. G. Rupp and P. S. Watson (Philadelphia: Westminster Press, 1969). For Luther's comparison of conscience to sexual organs, see *Works*, ed. J. Pelikan, vol. 27 (St Louis: Concordia, 1955–96). For Calvin's Institutes, see *Institution of Christian Religion*, tr. Thomas Norton, 1578 (EEBO). The full modern English text is available at <http://www.ccel.org/ccel/calvin/institutes> (accessed 31 January 2011).

I thank Katherine R. Cooper for introducing me to the sonnets of Anne Vaughan Lock. See http://newmedia.alma.edu/ottenhoff/psalm51/meditations.htm (accessed 31 January 2011).

Richard Hooker, *Of the Laws of Ecclesiastical Polity*, ed. Christopher Morris, vol. 1 (London: Everyman's Library, 1907).

Max Scheler, *Formalism in Ethics* (Evanston, IL: Northwestern University Press, 1973); *Person and Self-Value* (Dordrecht and Lancaster: Nijhoff, 1987).

Reinhold Niebuhr, *The Nature and Destiny of Man* (New York and London: Nisbet, 1941).

For Tillich, see below.

Chapter 2

For Locke's *Letter Concerning Toleration*, see http://www.constitution.org.jl/toleration.htm. For the *Essay Concerning Human Understanding*, see http://www.oreganstate.edu/instruct/phl302/texts/locke/locke1/Essay_contents.html (accessed 31 January 2011).

Anthony Ashley-Cooper, Earl of Shaftesbury, *Characteristiks of Men, Manners, Opinions, Times* (1737), vol. 2, sec 1. <http://www.oll .libertyfund.org/index> (accessed 31 January 2011).

Joseph Butler's celebrated 'cool hour' occurs in Sermon 11, *Fifteen Sermons Preached at the Rolls Chapel*, ed. W. R. Matthews (London, 1953).

Immanuel Kant, *The Metaphysics of Morals*, ed. Mary Gregor (Cambridge Texts in the History of Philosophy, 1996).

Adam Smith, *The Theory of Moral Sentiments*, ed. Knud Haaksonssen (Cambridge Texts in the History of Philosophy, 2002).

John Stuart Mill, *Essay on Liberty*: <http://etext.virginia.edu/toc/ modeng/public/MilLib2.html> (accessed 31 January 2011).

Chapter 3

Fyodor Dostoevsky, *Crime and Punishment*, tr. R. Pevear (London: Vintage Classics, 1993); *The Brothers Karamazov*, tr. R. Pevear (London: Everyman's Library, 1990).

Cathy Popkinhas assisted me with comments on the intimate relation of Russian *sovest* (etymologically, 'with' + 'knowledge') with Western (and, ultimately, Greek and Greek Orthodox) ideas of conscience.

Basic Writings of Nietzsche, tr. Walter Kaufmann (New York: Modern Library, 2000). On the letter to Overbeck, see Kaufmann, *Nietzsche: Philosopher, Psychologist, Antichrist* (Princeton: Princeton University Press, 1950).

Freud's various essays are found in the *Standard Edition of the Complete Psychological Works of Sigmund Freud*, tr. J. Strachey (London: Hogarth Press, 1953–74).

Chapter 4

Among many pertinent studies of conscientious objection are Peter Brock (ed.), *Records of Conscience: Three Autobiographical Narratives by Conscientious Objectors, 1665–1865* (York: William Sessions, 1993); John Rae, *Conscience and Politics: The British Government and the Conscientious Objector to Military Service, 1916–1919* (Oxford: Oxford University Press, 1970); A. Keim and G. Stoltzfus, *The Politics of Conscience: The Historical Peace Churches and America at War, 1917–1955* (Scottdale, PA: Herald

Press, 1988); Peter Brock (ed.), *Liberty and Conscience: A Documentary History of Conscientious Objectors in America through the Civil War* (Oxford: Oxford University Press, 2002). I am indebted to *Records of Conscience* for the instance of the objecting Quaker.

On 'conscience clauses', see especially Ben Smith, 'Coakley's Conscience Clause', *Politico*, 44, http://www.politico.com/blogs/bensmith/0110 (accessed 31 January 2011).

For the *Universal Declaration of Human Rights*, see http://www.un.org/en/documents/udhr (accessed 31 January 2011).

Alan Gewirth, *Human Rights: Essays on Justification* (Chicago: University of Chicago Press, 1982) contributed valuably to my thinking about this chapter. I am indebted to him for the Supreme Court citation. See also Henry Shue, *Basic Rights* (Princeton: Princeton University Press, 1996). For a lively discussion of 'rights' as a basis for justice, see Joseph R. Slaughter, *Human Rights, Inc* (New York: Fordham University Press, 2007).

R. Panikkar's discussion of Western concepts of civil liberty and their applicability to non-Western cultures appears in *Diogenes*, 120 (1982).

Hannah Arendt, *Eichmann in Jerusalem: A Report on the Banality of Evil* (London: Penguin, 1977).

William Tyndale, *Obedience of a Christian Man*, ed. David Daniell (London: Penguin, 2000). I thank Holly Crocker for bringing Tyndale to my attention.

For Hobbes on conscience, see *Leviathan*, ed. J. C. A. Gaskin (Oxford World's Classics, 1996), especially part 1, chapter 7. A stimulating blog by Stanley Fish adduces Hobbes as a proponent of public (versus private) conscience in relation to discussions of religiously based medical conscience clauses. In his acute analysis, Fish observes that 'one can (and should) relax the obligations of faith when one is not in church'. See *New York Times Opinion*, 12 April 2009: http://www.opinionator.blogs.nytimes.com/2009/04/12/conscience-vs-conscience (accessed 31 January 2011).

For Aquinas, see St Thomas Aquinas, *Summa Theologica*, tr. Fathers of the Dominican Province, vol. 1 (New York: Benziger Brothers, 1947), Part 1, Question 79, Article 13.

The commentator who wants 'a little human rights just now' is Slaughter, *Human Rights, Inc*, previously cited.

Chapter 5

Edward, Earl of Clarendon, *Miscellaneous Works*, 2nd edn. (London, 1751). I thank Laura Perille for this reference.

Augustine's *Confessions* is available in numerous editions; the Latin text is conveniently found in Loeb Classical Library, 2 vols (1989).

Robinson Crusoe is also widely available; see Oxford World's Classics, ed. Keymer et al. (2008).

'Markheim', *The Complete Short Stories of Robert Louis Stevenson*, ed. Barry Menikoff (New York: Modern Library, 2002).

Seventeenth-century works by Andrew Jones, Jeremiah Dyke, and John Jackson may be found in Early English Books Online (hereafter, EEBO).

For a discussion of conscience 'written on the heart', see Eric Jager, *The Book of the Heart* (Chicago: University of Chicago Press, 2000).

Pamela Gradon (ed.), *Ayenbite of Inwit*, Early English Text Society, Original Series, no. 278 (Oxford, 1987).

'Everyman', *Medieval Drama*, ed. David Bevington (Boston: Houghton Mifflin, 1975).

Martin Heidegger, *Being and Time*, tr. Joan Stambaugh (New York: SUNY Press, 1996).

Camus's characterization of Clamence is from *Charles Rolo*, 'Albert Camus: A Good Man', *The Atlantic Monthly* (May 1958), 32.

James Joyce, *A Portrait of the Artist as a Young Man* (London: Penguin, 1992).

On documentary photography, see Robert Coles, *Doing Documentary Work* (Oxford: Oxford University Press, 1997). For the agency of images, see W. J. T. Mitchell, *What Do Pictures Want?* (Chicago: University of Chicago Press, 2005).

The Sabrina Harman quotations are from Philip Gourevitch and Errol Morris, 'Exposure: The Woman Behind the Camera at Abu Ghraib', *New Yorker*, 28 March 2008. Also see Gourevitch and Morris, *The Ballad of Abu Ghraib* (New York: Penguin, 2009).

Wil S. Hylton, 'Prisoner of Conscience', appeared in *GQ* magazine, September 2006.

Susan Sontag, *On Photography* (New York: Anchor Books, 1990).

Boxed texts

The 'court' of conscience

In addition to works cited above, see J. Swift, 'On the Testimony of
Conscience', *Irish Tracts and Sermons*, ed. Louis Landa (Oxford:
Blackwell, 1948).

The Talking Cricket

The Pinocchio of C. Collodi, tr. J. T. Teehan (New York: Schocken
Books, 1985).

Gendering conscience

Jane Eyre is available in many editions; see Oxford World's Classics
(2008).

Conscience: troublemaker or second self?

See William Perkins, *A Discourse of Conscience*, 1596; Early English
Books Online. I thank Abraham Stoll for this reference.

Aquinas on conscience as 'applied knowledge'

Thomas Aquinas, *Summa Theologica*, Part 1, Question 79, Article 13.

Further reading

For the origins of conscience in legal pleading, I am indebted to C. A. Pierce, *Conscience in the New Testament* (London: SCM Press, 1955). This notably perceptive study abounds in fresh insights and is especially to be recommended.

Valuable observations on Christian traditions of conscience and the predicaments of conscience today are to be found in Paul Tillich, the 'Transmoral Conscience', in *Morality and Beyond* (New York: Harper Torchbooks, 1966), pp. 65–81.

For a fine discussion of conscience in Luther's early theology, see Michael G. Baylor, *Action and Person: Conscience in Late Scholasticism and the Young Luther* (Leiden: Brill, 1977). Some of the possible extremities of Protestant conviction are discussed by Steven E. Ozment, *Mysticism and Dissent: Religious Ideology and Social Protest in the Sixteenth Century* (New Haven and London: Yale University Press, 1973).

Many of the writings considered in my second chapter, together with other subjects of importance, are treated with impressive depth in Edward G. Andrew, *Conscience and Its Critics: Protestant Conscience, Enlightenment Reason, and Modern Subjectivity* (Toronto and London: University of Toronto Press, 2001). Highly recommended.

Especially pertinent to Kant, and also richly engaged with other themes treated in this book, is Thomas E. Hill, 'Four Conceptions of Conscience', *Human Welfare and Moral Worth: Kantian Perspectives* (Oxford: Oxford University Press, 2002).

Additional perspectives on issues treated here are to be found in
Charles Taylor, *Sources of the Self* (Cambridge: Cambridge
University Press, 1989) and Paul Ricoeur, *Oneself as Another*
(Chicago and London: University of Chicago Press, 1992).

Conscience

Index

Index

Expand your collection of
VERY SHORT INTRODUCTIONS

CHRISTIAN ETHICS
A Very Short Introduction
D. Stephen Long

This *Very Short Introduction* to Christian ethics introduces the topic by examining its sources and historical basis. D. Stephen Long presents a discussion of the relationship between Christian ethics, modern, and postmodern ethics, and explores practical issues including sex, money, and power. Long recognises the inherent difficulties in bringing together 'Christian' and 'ethics' but argues that this is an important task for both the Christian faith and for ethics. Arguing that Christian ethics are not a precise science, but the cultivation of practical wisdom from a range of sources, Long also discusses some of the failures of the Christian tradition, including the crusades, the conquest, slavery, inquisitions, and the Galileo affair.

www.oup.com/vsi

SOCIAL MEDIA
Very Short Introduction

Join our community
www.oup.com/vsi

- Join us online at the official Very Short Introductions **Facebook** page.
- Access the thoughts and musings of our authors with our online **blog**.
- Sign up for our monthly **e-newsletter** to receive information on all new titles publishing that month.
- Browse the full range of Very Short Introductions online.
- Read **extracts** from the Introductions for free.
- Visit our library of **Reading Guides**. These guides, written by our expert authors will help you to question again, why you think what you think.
- If you are a teacher or lecturer you can order inspection copies quickly and simply via our website.

ONLINE CATALOGUE
A Very Short Introduction

Our online catalogue is designed to make it easy to find your ideal Very Short Introduction. View the entire collection by subject area, watch author videos, read sample chapters, and download reading guides.